Myths of Social Media

Business Myths Series

Myths of Branding Simon Bailey and Andy Milligan
Myths of Leadership Jo Owen
Myths of Management Stefan Stern and Cary Cooper
Myths of Social Media Michelle Carvill and Ian MacRae
Myths of Strategy Jérôme Barthélemy
Myths of Work Ian MacRae

The above titles are available from all good bookshops.

For further information on these and other Kogan Page titles, or to order online, visit the Kogan Page website at: www.koganpage.com.

Michelle Carvill
Ian MacRae

MYTHS OF
SOCIAL MEDIA

Dispel the misconceptions and
master social media

2ND EDITION

KoganPage

First published in Great Britain and the United States in 2020 by Kogan Page Limited
Second edition published in 2023

2nd Floor, 45 Gee Street	8 W 38th Street, Suite 902	4737/23 Ansari Road
London	New York, NY 10018	Daryaganj
EC1V 3RS	USA	New Delhi 110002
United Kingdom		India

www.koganpage.com

Kogan Page books are printed on paper from sustainable forests.

© Michelle Carvill and Ian MacRae, 2020, 2023

The rights of Michelle Carvill and Ian MacRae to be identified as the authors of this work have been asserted by them in accordance with the Copyright, Designs and Patents Act 1988.

ISBNs
Hardback   978 1 3986 0780 4
Paperback   978 1 3986 0778 1
Ebook   978 1 3986 0779 8

British Library Cataloguing-in-Publication Data
A CIP record for this book is available from the British Library.

Library of Congress Cataloging-in-Publication Data
Names: Carvill, Michelle, 1969- author. | MacRae, Ian (Psychologist), author.
Title: Myths of social media : dispel the misconceptions and master social media / Michelle Carvill, Ian MacRae.
Description: 2nd Edition. | New York, NY : Kogan Page Inc, 2022. | Revised edition of the authors' Myths of social media, 2020. | Includes bibliographical references and index.
Identifiers: LCCN 2022031792 (print) | LCCN 2022031793 (ebook) | ISBN 9781398607781 (paperback) | ISBN 9781398607804 (hardback) | ISBN 9781398607798 (ebook)
Subjects: LCSH: Internet marketing. | Social media. | Information technology–Management.
Classification: LCC HF5415.1265 .C374 2022 (print) | LCC HF5415.1265 (ebook) | DDC 658.872–dc23/eng/20220801
LC record available at https://lccn.loc.gov/2022031792
LC ebook record available at https://lccn.loc.gov/2022031793

Typeset by Integra Software Services, Pondicherry
Print production managed by Jellyfish
Printed and bound by CPI Group (UK) Ltd, Croydon, CR0 4YY

For Marques and Jaiden Lui.
So I heard you like Mudkips?

Josephine and Eliza, your mumma is back
(for a while!) ;)

Contents

Introduction

There's no denying that, whether you love them or despise them, social media platforms have become a key component of our lives. You, your family members, your work colleagues and most definitely your customers, across a wide range of demographics and territories, are likely to tap into several different social media platforms every single day.

Such levels of adoption are hardly surprising. While the platforms are constantly evolving and advancing their technological competence on what seems like a monthly basis, some have been with us for 15–20 years. These flexible and creative communication and information resources are now firmly embedded in our day-to-day lives. Indeed, we have generations that don't know what life was like before social media. To them, connecting with friends and family via screens is totally normal.

Beyond entertainment and helping us navigate our lives, the platforms have become serious resources for businesses to engage and connect with key audiences, whether to nurture and build brand loyalty, or develop new audience attention. Social media is now a key component of how we connect, communicate and consume. It has many merits, such as real-time engagement and authentic conversation, audience and landscape insights, and the opportunity to listen in to audiences and gather market intelligence. But these merits can be detrimental for businesses and brands that ignore or misunderstand the 'two-way' accountability and expectation aspects of these social technologies.

Why we tackled the myths

As the platforms have pervaded our everyday lives, busi-nesses have naturally asked how they can optimize their presence. Like any new technology, there have been some significant teething problems over the years, with many stories of brands and organizations missing the point and getting into hot water. These are often widely reported in the press and on social media – and indeed whole books have been written about them. In *Myths of Social Media* we've tackled some of the most common misconceptions to support businesses in their use of social media. We settled on 30 myths, to ensure that we covered the most critical ones that specifically align with business activity. Each myth is structured to include background informa-tion and research that is useful to understand the different features and functions of social media for business and professional use.

Regardless of where you sit in your organization, whether you are CEO, founder, board member, manager, consultant, social media manager, executive, or a one-man/woman band going it alone, this book is designed to support you. Our hope is that it will help in two ways – to build wider awareness and understanding, and, impor-tantly, to give practical advice to support implementation, strategic and tactical planning and general optimization of the networks. Our aim is to improve the effectiveness of your social media activity.

How to use this book

Our best advice is to read through the book quickly in your first sitting before delving into any of the individual myths in detail, as there are stats, facts and insights that will support your wider understanding of how to utilize these platforms as key business resources. From the experience of talking to the many marketers and business owners we train, advise and consult with, we're aware that there is often still a need to build a business case to justify a wider remit, team or budget for social media activity. To this end, we've included myths such as 'Social media is a waste of time', 'Social media is free' and 'All social networks do the same thing'. These provide you with information and case studies to justify that business case. Oh, and let's not forget our myths 'Business leaders don't need a presence on social media' and 'Social media is not effective for business development'. Again, these can be used to support a strategic business case.

Each myth can stand alone: you can dip in and out and read any of them without having to read earlier ones in the book. But the myths are also interconnected and build on the recommendations and advice in other myths. This book is designed to be a quick reference on a range of topics. If you only have five minutes to make an important decision, pick it up and check the advice. Or if you're thinking through more complex or strategic problems, read through more myths in depth to look at the challenges and opportunities from different perspectives. Each myth is purposely succinct, giving you exactly what you need – with references and steers to explore further should you wish to.

We talk about a range of issues, from core operational priorities such as market segmentation and return on investment, to managing brand reputation, revealing trade secrets, data management and personal information you will think about in your day-to-day business. Then we talk about some of the broader social trends such as fake news, cancel culture, ownership of data, cybersecurity, and how social media affects users' perceptions and behaviour. These issues are tackled using a business and professionally oriented lens, and we discuss them from a practical and outcome-oriented perspective.

In a book about social technology it's hard not to get caught up in the moment. Rest assured, the bulk of our myths focus on the very real and timeless challenges all businesses face when it comes to navigating these flexible, multifaceted and widely used platforms.

For those looking for insights, you've got them; for those looking for practical support, it's in here. And for those looking for best practice and keeping ahead of the game, this one's for you...

Enjoy.

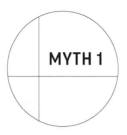

MYTH 1

Social media is a waste of time

Before assuming that social media is always a waste of time, ask the questions 'What do I want to achieve?' and 'Can social be used to help me achieve that goal?'

Is social media a waste of time? A study by Pew Research found that 82 per cent of Americans thought so.[1] However, that doesn't mean they're staying away from it. The same study reported that more people are now getting their news information from social media than from print media.

Most people, however, do use social media, irrespective of whether they think it is a good use of time. Pew reported that in 2021, 72 per cent of the US population had a social media profile, while 7 per cent didn't use the internet at all.[2,3] And in the UK, while the Office for National Statistics suggests that 96 per cent of the population have internet access, 70 per cent of the population use social media.[4,5]

All this is to say that, if social media is a waste of time, it has not stopped people from using it.

People waste time at work

It is necessary to distinguish between using social media for business or personal use. If someone spends most of their time after work scrolling through Facebook or Twitter, it is up to them to judge whether that time is wasted. However, if they spend time during their workday on personal social media to pass the time, or have private conversations, that almost certainly is time wasted if there is something else they ought to be doing.

Of course, there can be a bit of a grey area between personal social media use and work-related networking or 'fact finding' missions. For many careers, like journalists, recruiters, politicians and entertainers, social media is part of the job description. But, if someone feels the need to make an excuse for why they have been spending work hours on their personal social media, they probably were wasting time.

If the question was 'Do people waste time on social media?' the answer would certainly be a resounding 'yes'. But this problem is not unique to social media. There are few, if any, technologies, activities or tools that people can't find ways to pour endless amounts of their free time into. Whether that time is wasted, is a matter of values and perspective. Give the right person the right distraction, and you'll never hear from them again. Even time management software can be a waste of time: some people spend more time organizing and sprucing up their to-do lists than completing the tasks on the list.

People can waste time on social media at work, or anywhere at any time with the help of a smartphone with an internet connection. People can waste time watching TV, in the break room, on their phones. Even without any external distractions, employees can spend their time daydreaming instead of working.

There is nothing wrong with switching off from work – it is great to be able to when the time is appropriate and people will choose their own distractions and decide for themselves whether or not these are a good or bad use of time.[6] But for the purpose of this myth and much of this book, we want to discuss social media in the context of productivity and performance at work.

Yes, people can waste their own and their employer's time on social media at work – but there are also many ways in which social media can be a good use of time at work, and can actually be used to improve productivity, engagement and communication (Myth 13) sales (Myth 26), recruitment (Myth 21) and customer relations (Myths 6 and 12).

Above all, we need to recognize that there are perils and pitfalls to social media use – so we will be explaining what to watch out for, what to avoid and what to be cautious of in the subsequent myths. All applications of social media have risks as well as benefits. So before assuming that social media is always a waste of time, ask the questions 'What do I want to achieve?' and 'Can social media be used to help me achieve that goal?' With a bit of knowledge and creativity, it's amazing what can be accomplished using social media.

Social media forms a core component of communication in most people's digital lives. It is not just a hobby or a diversion, it is a foundational part of the world's information ecosystem and communications infrastructure.[7]

Weighing the benefits, risks and costs

The uses for social media at work are as varied as the business activities within and between companies. Some companies use social media for sales and marketing (Myths 7 and 27), others use it for recruiting new talent (Myth 21) and others have their own internal social networks (Myth 13).

Just because people waste time on computers or smartphones or social media, that doesn't mean that the technology is inherently a time-waster. If you're considering allowing the use of social media at work, instead of making vague generalizations, think about the specifics of how the technology will be used, and for what. There are 12 criteria that can be used to evaluate social media tools and platforms in the workplace:

1 **Purpose.** What is the technology going to be used for, and why? The purpose must be established upfront, and all subsequent issues can be weighed against how suitable the technology is for its purpose.

2 **Availability.** Who is the technology available to? Is it publicly available, or are there significant barriers to using it? Is it cost-effective and user-friendly enough for your business, employees or customers?

3 **Fitness for purpose.** How well does the technology fit with the purpose identified above? Some technologies fit

well enough, and some can be adapted. However, if the technology doesn't fit with the intended purpose or business outcomes, it could be a waste of time.

4 **Reliability.** How reliable is the technology? If there are frequent outages, technical problems or constant changes that make it unreliable, it may not be very useful.

5 **Maturity.** How well-developed is the technology? Advanced and well-tested systems tend to be more reliable and better developed to specific purposes. More popular platforms also tend to be easier for employees and customers to adopt because of their familiarity.

6 **Provenance.** How reputable is the technology or platform, who is the developer, and in which country is it based? For professional social networking, for example, established platforms and developers may be a better fit than obscure online forums.

7 **Support.** Does the platform or technology provide the necessary implementation and maintenance support? Is there anyone to contact if something goes wrong? If a company decides to outsource their communication, their networking, their performance management systems or similar processes to an external platform, there must be appropriate support available.

8 **Scalability.** Does the platform have the capacity to support your current and future requirements? It may be reasonable to move to a different platform if your requirements change, but it's wise to consider this in advance.

9 **Usability.** How easy and accessible is the platform for users? Introducing clunky, inefficient or confusing platforms may be counterproductive and lead to wasted time.

10 **Costs.** What are the potential costs (financial or otherwise) of using the technology and platform? If the purpose is clearly defined, the potential rewards (again, financial or otherwise) should be clear and can then be measured against costs.

11 **Risks.** What potential problems come with using the technology? There may be risks for the company's reputation or that of its employees, risks associated with customer data or with potential misuse of the platform. These frequently lead to unforeseen costs.

12 **Utility.** How do all these points add up? After weighing costs, risks and benefits against the purpose, it is possible to estimate the overall utility of the platform. Overall, is it worth using, or is there a better way of accomplishing the stated purpose?

Take the example of a company using a platform that is both an internal company social media network and a performance management system (this will be discussed in more detail in Myth 13). Its purpose is to be an internal communication network for employees that lets individuals track their own performance, while allowing colleagues to provide feedback and managers to track and record progress. There should be different levels of private, partially private and public information.

There are specific platforms that do exactly this. However, some of the more well-known social media platforms such as Facebook or LinkedIn might provide some of those features, but not all. The low cost and potential for scalability might be in these platforms' favour, but their fitness, risks and overall utility may not measure up.

These 12 factors may not all be equally important to you, depending on the platform's purpose, so in many cases it will make sense to focus on a few. For example, smaller businesses may want to test out new systems while prioritizing costs and reliability. Factors such as provenance and scalability may be less important in the short term. Ascertain whether a certain platform could be valuable, and if it matches up with the purpose for which you need it.

Opting out of social media

Do you still think social media is a complete waste of time? That's fine – you can always choose to opt out. But even if you have no desire to participate in anything related to social networking in the workplace, you should still read this book and understand how other people and companies are using it.

Perhaps you believe that social media is all well and good, has varied uses and benefits, but you just do not want to share any of your personal data with tech behemoths, internet service providers and/or corporate HQ. That's a perfectly reasonable option that some will choose. But if you or your company opt out, you will need to find other ways to be competitive and productive. You still need to understand how your colleagues or competitors are operating, and what they are doing well.

Conclusion

Anything can be a waste of time when it is used incorrectly – this is not a problem particular to social media. If you want to take an analytical approach, look at those 12 criteria and decide which are most important to you. Ask yourself whether the time you're spending on social media is helping you achieve your personal or professional goals.

Notes

1   Social media outpaces print newspapers in the U.S. as a news source: http://www.pewresearch.org/fact-tank/2018/12/10/social-media-outpaces-print-newspapers-in-the-u-s-as-a-news-source (archived at https://perma.cc/W7QQ-9Q9F)

2   Social media fact sheet: https://www.pewresearch.org/internet/fact-sheet/social-media/ (archived at https://perma.cc/YM4G-CWG6)

3   7% of Americans don't use the internet. Who are they? https://www.pewresearch.org/fact-tank/2021/04/02/7-of-americans-dont-use-the-internet-who-are-they/ (archived at https://perma.cc/D5AS-2RHR)

4   Internet access – households and individuals, Great Britain: 2020: www.ons.gov.uk/peoplepopulationandcommunity/householdcharacteristics/homeinternetandsocialmediausage/bulletins/internetaccesshouseholdsandindividuals/2020 (archived at https://perma.cc/77V6-DX6Q)

5   Social network user penetration in the UK from 2017 to 2026: www.statista.com/statistics/553582/predicted-social-network-user-penetration-rate-in-the-united-kingdom-uk/ (archived at https://perma.cc/N5H7-ZFFS)

6   MacRae, I and Furnham, A (2017) *Motivation and Performance: A guide to motivating a diverse workforce*, Kogan Page, London

7   MacRae, I (2021) *Dark Social: Understanding the darker side of work, personality and social media*, Bloomsbury, London

MYTH 2

All social networks do the same thing

As the channels have evolved, so too has consumer adoption. The ever-expanding range of features offered has given business more reasons to get involved with more channels.

Communication is a complex beast. What, why and how we communicate differs from person to person, situation to situation, culture to culture, and indeed nation to nation. And not only do cultural and behavioural aspects come into play, but so too does the all-important situational context.

When it comes to who is using social media channels and for what purpose, plenty of continuously updated sources of information provide the latest user statistics. The Digital 2022 report from We Are Social[1] is an excellent, annually updated source of global insight into our digital and social media behaviour, motivation and engagement.

While user demographics and motivations vary from platform to platform, what is clear is that we're at a mass saturation point when it comes to users accessing social media. The report outlines that 98 per cent of digital consumers are social media users, with an average of 7.5 social media accounts, up from 4.8 in 2014. The number of accounts correlates with user needs. For example, a person may have:

- their personal profile on Facebook which they use to communicate with friends and family;
- a LinkedIn profile for their own professional personal brand which they use for thought leadership and connecting with clients, influencers and prospects;
- a company profile which is the voice of their organization.

The role social media now plays in our lives is multifaceted and has significantly evolved beyond simple networking. Smartphones have become an extension of our everyday lives, enabling the evolution of social platforms into key entertainment and e-commerce platforms.

While social channels may have similar functionality to one another, it's interesting not only to observe your own preferences and behaviour, but also to draw on global research to better understand just how differently we've embraced the channels to serve different purposes. The fact that people online have an average of 7.5 social media accounts begs the question – why? In this chapter, we'll explore whether all social media channels are the same, taking a closer look at how the most popular channels are being used, and how usage differs from channel to channel.

Twitter

Quick stats:[2]

- 5.1 hours (average time per month that users spend on the platform)
- 3.3 per cent of internet users aged 16–64 state Twitter is their favourite platform
- 436 million global active users

While the Facebook family 'Meta', including Facebook, Instagram and WhatsApp, dominate social media usage, some 436 million people use Twitter daily. This equates to over 500 million tweets being sent each day – approximately 6,000 tweets every second.[3]

Due to the sheer volume of tweets, the crafting of messages tends to adhere to the philosophy 'be brief, be bold, be gone'. The floozy of the social networks, tweets don't stick around for long, as Twitter feeds are constantly refreshing. In fact, when search engine optimization specialists MOZ undertook research to identify the average lifespan of a tweet, they found it to be around just 18 minutes.[4]

Whether people are following their interests or tuned in to what people are talking about generally, the social network is generally viewed as a trusted news source. In fact, most news breaks on Twitter.

Generally, Twitter offers a simple and quick way to keep your eye on the ball on topics you're interested in. An effective search function enables users to search via hashtags or keywords to find latest trends, updates and insights. The brevity of the messages means that you can quickly skim through your feed and gain a general gist of what's happening – as it happens. From a business perspective, this enables you not only to share what's going on in your own business, but, importantly, to keep up to speed with what's going on in the business landscape, keeping a keen eye on markets, competitors, influencers, customers and potential customers. Beyond organic activity, as with most of the social networks, Twitter enables a powerful advertising platform for brands and organizations to target audiences with campaigns and messaging via sophisticated targeting options.

LinkedIn

Quick stats:[5,6]

- 310 million – total number of monthly active users
- 690 million – total number of professionals on LinkedIn
- 808.4 million – total potential reach of ads on LinkedIn

Individuals tend to use LinkedIn for professional networking, making new connections, personal brand development, business developments and job searching. Companies use it for employer brand, recruitment, business development and sharing company information with current and prospective employees. It's the ultimate online directory of business professionals and organizations, enabling network members to manage their current connections and add new ones to their professional networks.

For organizations, LinkedIn offers an extension of their corporate website, with the ability to share latest news and updates from within the organization. It's useful for employee engagement, keeping internal team members in the loop, as well as PR, marketing and business development.

The LinkedIn corporate profile is a central hub for connected employees to source and share relevant articles and news – helping to amplify content by sharing it with their networks. It also gives organizations an opportunity to disseminate internal news; new products, services and developments to be shared with a wider audience, both organically and again, via sophisticated targeted paid advertising opportunities.

For the individual, having a LinkedIn profile is almost a rite of professional passage. People expect professionals to be available on the platform. Beyond an online CV, it offers the opportunity to create a professional online presence, showcasing personal brand, values, skills, expertise, experience and credibility.

From the various reports highlighted, job hunting and recruitment, marketing and PR, and business networking are most certainly key aspects of why people use LinkedIn. It's a reliable source of professional content too.

Facebook

Quick stats:[7]

- 19.6 hours (average time per month that users spend on the platform)

- 14.5 per cent of internet users aged 16–64 state Facebook is their favourite platform
- 2.91 billion global active users

Facebook is the world's largest social network, with 2.91 billion global active users. It started as a means for keeping in touch with friends and family and sharing updates, photos and videos. While those aspects are still relevant, the platform has evolved into a powerful advertising platform where paid reach dominates.

Beyond the Facebook personal profile or company page, Facebook has a wider ecosystem. Facebook Groups enable the development of open and closed communities, and Facebook Messenger, a private and group messaging system, offers individuals, brands and organizations a way to liaise in real time. This can happen through customized chatbot features, opening up conversations when a user clicks on an ad, sending targeted messages to groups of contacts or directly integrating with e-commerce stores to support customer experience and purchases. Given that research from Sprout Social named responsiveness on social media as the number one factor influencing consumers to purchase, Facebook Messenger's features can significantly help in moving buyers along the purchase consideration funnel.[8]

As well as the organic aspects of Facebook such as networking, the platform dominates digital paid advertising, offering unparalleled granular audience targeting for brands, retail organizations and businesses of all shapes and sizes. The opportunity to direct highly targeted marketing messages straight to specific audiences is something we'll explore further in Myth 3.

Facebook advertising (which includes Instagram placements) most certainly plays a role in influencing individuals, and therefore the purchase journey. The Digital 2022 report states that 43.5 per cent of people use social media to research new brands or products, making this the second most important channel overall – and among the 16–24 age group social media comes top, overtaking traditional search engines.[9]

WhatsApp

Quick stats:[10]

- 2 billion global monthly active users
- 15.7 per cent of internet users aged 16–64 choose WhatsApp as their favourite social network
- 18.6 hours – average time per month users spend on the platform

WhatsApp is unique in several ways, compared to other social networks. Part of the 'Meta' family, it was originally developed to allow users to privately send messages, video and images to each other through their smartphones. It provides a free alternative to SMS (text messaging) which – depending on tariffs – is often still a pay-per-use service. Not only is WhatsApp often more cost-effective than SMS, but it facilitates large group conversations; something that is difficult through SMS, if not impossible.

WhatsApp for Business was launched in January 2018. Positioned as a resource for the small business owner and the mobile app, it enables businesses to interact with customers in just the same way as with the original app.

Generally, WhatsApp is used for group chats – whether that's family, friends, interest groups or teams within organizations.

Snapchat

Quick stats:[11]

- 557 million – global monthly active users
- 3 hours – average time per month users spend on the platform
- 1.4 per cent of internet users aged 16–64 choose Snapchat as their favourite social network

Snapchat, once courted by 'Meta', remains an independent mobile app messenger service that allows people to express themselves, sharing pictures and videos in the moment that disappear after 10 seconds.

Snapchat were the pioneers of augmented reality fun filters, providing hours of engagement. The platform also pioneered the 24-hour 'story' feature (now commonplace across Facebook, Instagram and even LinkedIn). In the same way that Instagram Stories stick around once saved to Highlights, when saved to Memories, Snapchat content can live on longer than the 24-hour deadline.

In comparison to Instagram and WhatsApp messenger services, Snapchat comes in a distant third. However, it does see much higher usage figures in North America, particularly among 16–24-year-olds.

When it comes to business benefits, Snapchat has its uses, again with sophisticated paid advertising, particularly when targeting the youth market. For example, Amazon regularly uses Snapchat for key promotions such as Black Friday, providing Snapchat-only promotional codes to access deals. This creates a sense of exclusivity for its Snapchat followers.[12]

Youtube

Quick stats:[13]

- 23.7 hours – average time per month users spend on the platform
- 2.6 billion global monthly active users

Part of Google, YouTube is currently the largest free video-sharing service in the world, where users can create a profile, upload videos and watch, like and comment on other videos.

Cited as a strong second to Facebook's dominant social platform position, YouTube is perfect for brand building, thought leadership and sharing practical advice. The platform effectively gives individuals, brands and organizations the opportunity to develop their own TV station. And, as with Facebook, Instagram, LinkedIn and Twitter, users can livestream video directly via YouTube.

If we look at visitor numbers per month, YouTube takes the top position. It's the only major social network to have more unregistered visitors than logged-in members. This means that significant numbers of visitors don't bother to log in to their account – or possibly don't even have one. This quirk of user behaviour makes YouTube less a social network and (in the same vein as Google's search engine) more of a social hub – accessible to all, regardless of whether they have an active account.

Heralded as the second largest search engine in the world, Brandwatch reports that 6 out of 10 people prefer watching video on YouTube rather than TV.[14] In fact, 18–49-year-olds now spend less time watching TV, while time on YouTube has increased by 74 per cent. On mobile alone, YouTube reaches more 18–49-year-olds than any other broadcast or cable TV network. On average, there are more than 1,000,000,000 mobile video views per day.

Many individual 'influencers' have rocketed to superstardom broadcasting on the channel. The top 20 most searched channels on YouTube are largely influential 'tubers' who have built significant audiences for their entertaining content, achieving fame – and sometimes fortune.[15]

From a business perspective, the channel is fully embraced as a medium to blend entertainment and commerce. Organically, it offers the opportunity to showcase real-world footage, behind-the-scenes insights, product launches, how-to tutorials, expert voices and thought leadership and, of course, entertainment. And of course, a significant part of its appeal is, again, the paid advertising targeting options.

Instagram

Quick stats:[16]

- 11.2 hours – average time per month users spend on the platform
- 1.5 billion – global monthly active users
- 14.8 per cent of internet users aged 16–64 choose Instagram as their favourite social network

Part of the 'Meta' family, Instagram is predominantly a mobile app which offers a fast and simple way to share images and live video with followers.

Instagram has several features, for example IGTV, which enables live video streaming. Videos can be saved to create a 'video hub' accessible for replays and brand building – much in the same way as YouTube. The 'Stories' feature allows users to provide behind-the-scenes commentary on what's happening within an organization or brand via images and short video. This is separate to the main feed (often referred to as 'the grid'). This feature allows you to share real-world, fly-on-the-wall content which makes it perfect for driving engagement and building audience. It's also great for sharing product launches, events and, of course, promotions. Instagram Stories last for 24 hours, but can be saved to Highlights, adding longevity to real-world events to assist with branding and awareness via the main profile. 'Guides' have also been developed, which enable content and posts to be curated into useful collective documents, as well as providing features, such as 'reels', to spice up the content to make it more appealing and engaging.

Hashtags rule on Instagram. Up to 30 hashtags can be used on each post to maximize reach and opportunity to connect with relevant conversations, trends and audiences. Up to 10 hashtags can be used within each 'story'. From a user perspective, searching via hashtags allows you to find new posts or accounts aligned with particular hashtags, or see which hashtags are trending.

Being a mobile app and as part of the Facebook Ads Platform, Instagram also allows brands and organizations to drive powerful targeted campaigns, both organically and via paid advertising campaigns, directly into the palms of receptive individuals.

TikTok

Quick stats:[17]

- 19.6 hours – average time per month users spend on the platform
- 1 billion – global monthly active users
- 4.3 per cent of internet users aged 16–64 choose TikTok as their favourite social network

TikTok is a social app used to create and share videos. It differs from other platforms, in that video is the only content format. Most video content tends to be music-focused or linked to music – as the app boasts a vast catalogue of sound effects. Users tend to post short clips that include dancing or lip-synching – covering fun, education, entertainment and social causes. The platform has high user engagement, and from a perspective of hours per month on the platform, it's on a par with the leader, Facebook.

With a focus on brevity, videos can be up to 15 seconds long, but can be connected to other clips for up to 60 seconds (which was extended to three minutes in 2021).

While initially a refuge of fun, laughter, influencer engagement and play for younger generations, the platform is starting to broaden its appeal to businesses for brand building, awareness and e-commerce – particularly when it comes to its targeted and varied ad placement advertising opportunities. In 2021 TikTok and Shopify announced TikTok Shopping – an in-app e-commerce shopping experience that lets brands sell products on TikTok. Given that according to the Digital 2022 report, 27.7 per cent of internet users aged 16–64 use social media platforms to find inspiration for things to buy, the platform is not to be ignored.

Conclusion

It is not true that all social networks do the same thing. As the channels have evolved, so too has consumer adoption. The ever-expanding range of features offered has given business more reasons to get involved with more channels.

We needed to be selective with the ones that we chose to discuss in this myth. There wasn't room to include Discord, Reddit and Quora – three forum-style social networks which see millions of people converging in discussion around specific topics. The key is to identify the nuances within each network and understand which align with your audiences, organizational needs and objectives.

Notes

1   Digital 2022 We Are Social Report: https://wearesocial.com/uk/blog/
    2022/01/digital-2022/ (archived at https://perma.cc/KNN4-AGZT)
2   Twitter statistics and trends: https://datareportal.com/essential-twitter-
    stats (archived at https://perma.cc/6NDV-LMAK)
3   33 Twitter stats that matter to marketers in 2022: https://blog.
    hootsuite.com/twitter-statistics/ (archived at https://perma.cc/2V9Z-
    LMHQ)
4   When is my tweet's prime of life? (A brief statistical interlude): https://
    moz.com/blog/when-is-my-tweets-prime-of-life (archived at https://
    perma.cc/PB4S-ZPCH)
5   81 LinkedIn statistics you need to know in 2022: https://www.
    omnicoreagency.com/LinkedIn-statistics/ (archived at https://perma.cc/
    ZBY6-N375)
6   Digital 2022 We Are Social Report: https://wearesocial.com/uk/blog/
    2022/01/digital-2022/ (archived at https://perma.cc/KNN4-AGZT)
7   Digital 2022 We Are Social Report: https://wearesocial.com/uk/blog/
    2022/01/digital-2022/ (archived at https://perma.cc/KNN4-AGZT)
8   The Sprout Social Index, Edition XI: Social personality: https://
    sproutsocial.com/insights/data/q2-2017 (archived at https://perma.
    cc/3QFK-Y8UJ)
9   Digital 2022 We Are Social Report: https://wearesocial.com/uk/
    blog/2022/01/digital-2022/ (archived at https://perma.cc/KNN4-
    AGZT)
10 Digital 2022 We Are Social Report: https://wearesocial.com/uk/
    blog/2022/01/digital-2022/ (archived at https://perma.cc/KNN4-
    AGZT)
11 Digital 2022 We Are Social Report: https://wearesocial.com/uk/
    blog/2022/01/digital-2022/ (archived at https://perma.cc/KNN4-
    AGZT)
12 7 Brands that are killing it on Snapchat: www.entrepreneur.com/
    article/286147 (archived at https://perma.cc/9ZTU-MBXS)
13 Digital 2022 We Are Social Report: https://wearesocial.com/uk/blog/
    2022/01/digital-2022/ (archived at https://perma.cc/KNN4-AGZT)

14 57 fascinating and incredible YouTube statistics: www.brandwatch.
    com/blog/youtube-stats/ (archived at https://perma.cc/6JVH-KQRG)

15 2019's top YouTube searches and channels (so far): www.
    searchenginejournal.com/2019s-top-youtube-searches-and-channels-
    so-far/290569 (archived at https://perma.cc/WB28-8JUJ)

16 Digital 2022 We Are Social Report: https://wearesocial.com/uk/blog/
    2022/01/digital-2022/ (archived at https://perma.cc/KNN4-AGZT)

17 Digital 2022 We Are Social Report: https://wearesocial.com/uk/blog/
    2022/01/digital-2022/ (archived at https://perma.cc/KNN4-AGZT)

Social media isn't that influential

Not only has social media pervaded our lives as a means of communication and entertainment, it's a growing influencer when it comes to inspiring our purchasing decisions and business partnerships.

Whether we like it or not, digital has totally pervaded our everyday lives. We're not just living in a digital age, but so too a 'social media age', in which 98 per cent of digital consumers are social network users, according to the Digital 2022 report. The same annual research report, which tracks internet and social media usage, identifies that the number of internet users worldwide is 4.95 billion. Comparatively, and contrary to some news reports that social media usage is waning, the number of social media users worldwide is 4.62 billion – up 12 per cent over the past decade. The report also found that we spend approximately two hours and 27 minutes of our time on social media channels each day and among the 16–24-year-old demographic this is even higher, having just reached three hours and 13 minutes.[1]

Not too many years ago, social media was dismissed as the latest fad, yet adoption and dependency continue to rise. In this myth, we explore just how influential social media channels have become.

Social media and consumer influence

According to research from Sprout Social, 74 per cent of shoppers – both business to consumer (B2C) and business to business (B2B) – make buying decisions based on information on social media.[2] Similarly, the PwC Global Consumer Insights Survey named social media as the most influential channels for inspiring purchases (more so than websites, review sites, direct mail, email, comparison sites, press advertising and many others).[3]

As discussed in Myth 2, social media is now an integral part of product research, with around 40 per cent of people using social media to research new brands or products. In the younger demographic (the 16–24-year-olds), according to the Digital 2022 report, social media comes top, over-taking traditional search engines.[4]

Research from Global Web Index cites that 98 per cent of consumers globally say they've visited a social network in the past month, and 27 per cent state they use social platforms primarily to research and find products to buy, (only slightly less than the figure for TV ads at 31 per cent) and 26 per cent saying they tend to buy brands they see advertised.[5]

Take a moment to reflect and consider your own purchasing behaviour and how influenced you are by consumer reviews, for example on sites such as Airbnb, TripAdvisor and Amazon or indeed in the comments sections of social media ads. It's likely that with a quick scroll on your phone, you too have been swayed by the wisdom of the crowd.

And it transpires that what we're looking to purchase also has a bearing on where we turn for influence. A McKinsey report found that the degree of impact varies depending on what is being purchased.[6] Their study found that for utility products, 15 per cent of respondents reported using social media to assist with their purchase, whereas for other categories such as travel, investment services and over-the-counter drugs from pharmacies, the percentage increased to around 40–50 per cent. Their study also found a relationship with loyalty – first-time purchasers were 50 per cent more likely to turn to social media for recommendations than a repeat buyer.

Direct sales on social

What's interesting to note is that while there's clear evidence that our purchasing decisions are influenced by social media, social media channels are not the preferred choice for making the actual sale.

As reported in the Global Web Index research, social media plays a big role in the buying journey right up to the point of purchase, but the appetite to complete the transaction directly via social media platforms remains low – with many users preferring to switch across to the retail site. However, the same report showcases that Meta reports more than 1 billion Facebook users access Marketplace each month, and Instagram Shop has already started to gain momentum, reporting that advertisers can now reach more than 187 million users with ads in the Shop tab each month. So momentum around social commerce continues to grow.

Pinterest also has 'Buy now' buttons, and many highly targeted social advertising campaigns have been run across the platforms, encouraging users to buy directly via their site. The Digital 2022 report highlights that currently only 12 per cent say that a 'Buy' button on social media encourages them to make a purchase.

The Digital 2022 report outlines evidence that in China, social media as a direct commerce platform is highly successful. Whether there are inherent cultural differences impacting the general reluctance to buy via social in the West, or other factors at play, it will be interesting to see whether social media moving towards more of an entertainment and shopping function, together with the increased ease of in-app purchasing, will in time move the direct sales needle. Our prediction is that it will.

The influencer marketing industry

As discussed more widely in Myth 18, not only has social media pervaded our lives as a means of communication and entertainment, it's also enabled individuals to become social superstars. 'Social influencers' is a term used to describe individuals who have built a significant fan base via social media. Fame, once only afforded to pop stars, movie stars, sports stars or TV celebrities, is within the reach of 'ordinary' people.

Social media has given a golden opportunity to anyone who wants to build their own brand and influence online. Whether it's arts and crafts, gaming, singing, skateboarding, BMX stunting, comedy or unboxing, charisma and passion chimes with audiences, and significantly increases engagement. These often large and highly engaged fan bases have created a whole new influencer marketing industry. Just as we trust our friends and family via social media, so too do we trust these highly engaged strangers.

For example, if an influencer, whether sponsored or not, shares a post speaking favourably about a pair of trainers and tagging the product or including a link, it's likely that those following them will at the very least check out the product and may seek to purchase. According to the Digital Marketing Institute, 49 per cent of consumers follow influencer recommendations, and 40 per cent had purchased something after seeing it on Twitter, YouTube or Instagram.[7]

Social media advertising

It's also worth considering how social media advertising is influencing our purchases and actions. We touch on the effect of targeted advertising and messaging in Myth 5, and discuss the highly negative impact this can sometimes have. There's no denying that advertising on social media has become highly sophisticated. The data insights and real-time tracked consumer behaviours and preferences provide advertisers with granular demographics and insights to effect hyper-targeted and relevant messaging.

From a traditional marketing and sales perspective, social media proliferates at every point of the traditional consideration funnel, from awareness all the way through to advocacy.

Social media's relationship with the smartphone is not to be underestimated. As reported in the Digital 2022 report, 90 per cent of social media activity is executed via mobile[8] – and let's face it, we're all addicted to our mobile phones, which significantly boosts the success of social's advertising messages. It's difficult to name any other advertising platform that offers the same level of granular targeting, reach, and the ability to send timely messages directly into the palms of our hands.

Building communities

Beyond using social media to directly sell products or services, organizations are also turning to social networks to build powerful communities. The use of ad blockers is on the rise. Increasing numbers of consumers are switching off the noise of traditional push advertising. This, coupled with the rise of the 'belief-driven buyer', means that more consumers, brands and organizations are harnessing the power of social media to build relationships rather than to advertise.[9] They use it to engage on a more personal level, not only to build loyalty, but to educate their audiences and encourage them to share experiences, support one another and come together to develop change initiatives.

For example, the Global Consumer Insights Survey describes how Under Armour has developed an online fitness community encouraging its customers to share content across their range of social media, joined by Under Armour athletes such as former number one golfer Jordan Spieth. Patagonia, the outdoor clothing and accessories brand, has built a community around its core brand values aligned with environmental causes – educating customers to consider the environmental impact of their purchases.

Conclusion

Contrary to the title of this myth, social media is becoming increasingly influential. Not only has it pervaded our lives as a means of communication and entertainment, it's a growing influencer when it comes to inspiring our purchasing decisions and business partnerships. The internet, social media and mobile are inextricably linked – which is having a considerable impact on not only our lives, but also the consumer journey.

Notes

1   Digital 2022 We Are Social Report: https://wearesocial.com/uk/blog/
    2022/01/digital-2022/ (archived at https://perma.cc/KNN4-AGZT)

2 How social media is influencing purchase decisions: https://
   socialmediaweek.org/blog/2017/05/social-media-influencing-purchase-
   decisions (archived at https://perma.cc/CLQ7-LJ4A)

3 Global Consumer Insights Survey 2018: Whom Do Customers Really
   Trust? www.pwc.com/gx/en/retail-consumer/assets/consumer-trust-
   global-consumer-insights-survey.pdf (archived at https://perma.cc/
   ENR4-ACGS)

4 Digital 2022 We Are Social Report: https://wearesocial.com/uk/
   blog/2022/01/digital-2022/ (archived at https://perma.cc/KNN4-AGZT)

5 How effective are ads on social media? https://blog.gwi.com/trends/
   ads-on-social-media/ (archived at https://perma.cc/E3H2-7TE2)

6 Getting a sharper picture of social media's influence: www.mckinsey.
   com/business-functions/marketing-and-sales/our-insights/getting-a-
   sharper-picture-of-social-medias-influence (archived at https://perma.cc/
   3F7E-ULP5)

7 20 Influencer Marketing Statistics that will Surprise You: https://
   digitalmarketinginstitute.com/en-gb/blog/20-influencer-marketing-
   statistics-that-will-surprise-you (archived at https://perma.cc/AQ5C-
   ABHR)

8 Digital 2022 We Are Social Report: https://wearesocial.com/uk/
   blog/2022/01/digital-2022/ (archived at https://perma.cc/XP7Z-6449)

9 2018 Edelman Earned Brand: Brands Take a Stand: www.edelman.com/
   sites/g/files/aatuss191/files/2018-10/2018_Edelman_Earned_Brand_
   Global_Report.pdf (archived at https://perma.cc/NB6R-6UEV)

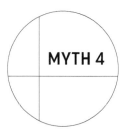

Social media replaces real-life networking

Social networking doesn't replace face-to-face networking. Instead, it complements it, and helps to start and deepen relationships.

When evaluating this myth, it's worth us revisiting the very beginning of social media.

Step back two decades to when they first began: LinkedIn in 2002, Facebook in 2004 and Twitter in 2006. At this time, each platform was regularly referred to as a 'social networking' platform. In fact, in their own biographies they still are. The focus was about connecting with friends, family and social networking – making new connections, digitally. Effectively, it was old-school networking revisited online.

The evolution of social media platforms since their networking foundations includes the development of sophisticated advertising methodologies – the ability to supply timely content and advertisements straight into the palms of highly targeted audiences. Paid social media has become a central part of social media strategy, not only aligned with e-commerce potential, but also to help brands and organizations optimize reach. Brands and organizations are no longer reliant on organic networked conversations, referrals and sharing among their followers, but instead, in line with algorithms and their limiting organic reach, they have to take advantage of a range of advertising options to target audiences directly.

In this myth, we'll consider the values of traditional networking alongside the ongoing debate around whether social networking replaces traditional networking – or whether they're the perfect complementary partners.

Both sides of the argument

When writing the first edition of *Myths of Social Media*, at Debate.org, there was an online debate under way discussing whether online social networking could replace face-to-face interaction. At the time of writing this second edition, the debate no longer exists. To summarize the main views, the Yes voters believed that social media:

- enables those who wouldn't ordinarily speak up in a room due to shyness to air their views;
- enables connection with a wider community that people wouldn't ordinarily have access to;
- enables people to access and explore wider viewpoints without the constraint of geography;

- gives access to more opinion and expertise, help and advice;
- enables people to use their time more effectively and stay in tune with people they don't ordinarily have time to.

Despite these points, the findings showed a consensus, even among the Yes voters, that meeting face-to-face is generally better. There was also general agreement that face-to-face meetings aren't always possible, and that social networks can help fill that void and enable connectivity and collaboration, albeit remotely, where otherwise there may have been a total loss of communication.

This played out in the Covid-19 pandemic, when social networking became a principal way of communicating and connecting in both our personal and professional lives. At the time of writing, we've moved out of physical restrictions in the UK, but the levels of remote working, remote events, remote meetings, and digital connectivity and social networking, have remained higher than ever.[1]

Online and offline relationships

A study carried out by *MIT Technology Review* found that when personal relationships start online, they may have an advantage over relationships that start in real life.[2] The report focused on a body of research which has been studying the concept of social networks for 50 years. It shows that real social networks are those where people are strongly connected to a relatively small group of neighbours and only loosely connected to more distant people. (We liken this to friends and family and acquaintances.)

In the study, the 'loose connections' turn out to be extremely important, serving as a bridge between our close friends and other groups, enabling us to connect with a wider community.

From the personal relationship perspective, it's the loose connections that have traditionally played a key role in meeting our partners. While most people were unlikely to date one of their best friends, they were highly likely to date people who they met though a friend of a friend. In the language of network theory, dating partners were embedded in one another's networks.

Turning to the online networks, then, the report explores how online dating has changed that language of network theory – for the better. People who meet online tend to be complete strangers – and when people meet in this way, it sets up social links that were previously non-existent. There are many benefits being reaped due to the introduction of these new social links – one being that it offers a broader opportunity to break away from the potential confines of our own local networks.

Another interesting finding from the research is that married couples who meet online have lower rates of marital break-up than those who meet through more traditional avenues. This is likely because selection criteria within social networks are quite targeted, so those meeting tend to share more of the same values.

Parallels with business networking

While we couldn't find any similar studies that have been formally carried out in the business arena, given that we're all human beings, from a relationship development perspective, we can use this lens to look at the development of business relationships. In just the same way that social networks are facilitating new social links that wouldn't ordinarily happen in the dating world, so too are they facilitating new links in the business world. For example, platforms such as CoFounders Lab help those seeking business partners to access over 400,000 potential matches.[3]

Networking has always played a significant role in business development. LinkedIn, probably the social network most synonymous with online business networking, focuses its entire platform on helping businesspeople to connect, expand and strengthen their professional networks. It operates a tiered level of connection – primary connections, secondary connections and third-tier connections. Primary connections are those in your immediate network – these may be your peers, people you regularly do business with, or people you've met and have decided to connect with for ongoing conversation and future opportunity. The secondary network are those that your primary network are connected to, and the third tier are those that are yet to be reached through your network.

LinkedIn provides clear visibility of where people sit in your network. For example, let's say you're at a business event and you meet someone. You decide to connect with them on LinkedIn, search for them on the platform, and see that they are a secondary connection, already connected to your sales director. Immediately, this gives you the opportunity to open a conversation about the strength and context of that relationship.

This feature can also be useful for making network connections more indirectly. Using the same example, let's say you're at that business event, and you see someone speaking on stage. You decide they would be a great connection for business development. You don't know them, you haven't spoken to them, yet when you search for them on the platform, you notice that your sales director is already connected to them. You could then ask your sales director to introduce the two of you – in just the same way they may make an introduction offline. We explore the concept of using social networking for business development, commonly referred to as 'social selling', in more detail in Myth 15.

Moving from online to offline (without the awkwardness)

Some people love face-to-face networking. They happily attend events with the objective of making as many connections as possible. For others, break times at events with facilitated 'space to network' can be an excruciatingly awkward affair causing people to bury their heads in their phones or spend longer than necessary in the bathroom.

When it comes to moving from online to offline networking, it's always a little less socially awkward to meet with someone you've been talking to online. There's already a shared sense of 'knowing them' – the icebreakers have happened, and you're often into a different level of conversation. Research in *Science Daily* supports this notion, showing that the online world is now increasingly facilitating new relationships in the offline world.[4]

It's useful at this point to address your own use of online and offline networking – and reflect on the realities. While you may have hundreds or perhaps thousands of connections online, it's highly likely that you're in regular contact with only a few people at any one time.

Those conversations and connections are generally clustered around a shared interest or topic. And if you join in a conversation around a shared interest or topic, it may be that you find yourself interacting with a new 'social link' – who just so happens to be on the same wavelength or has a slightly different view which you find interesting – and so you connect. What starts online may even evolve into a long-standing, relevant and strong relationship.

Conclusion

Social networking doesn't replace face-to-face networking. Instead, it complements it, and helps to start and deepen relationships, either via continuous conversations, shared online or offline initiatives, or a move towards face-to-face meetings or a collaborative project.

Notes

1   The future of work after COVID-19: https://www.mckinsey.com/
    featured-insights/future-of-work/the-future-of-work-after-covid-19
    (archived at https://perma.cc/RP7M-J4FP)
2   First evidence that online dating is changing the nature of society: www.
    technologyreview.com/s/609091/first-evidence-that-online-dating-is-
    changing-the-nature-of-society/ (archived at https://perma.cc/35FR-VTNR)

3 CoFounders Lab: www.cofounderslab.com (archived at https://perma.cc/ 8JQH-T6S6)

4 Online and offline: The changing face of meetings: www.sciencedaily.com/ releases/2015/03/150309082814.htm (archived at https://perma.cc/ P89B-TAAZ)

MYTH 5

Social media marketing is a dark art

Social media can be used to sell everything from useless products to toxic ideologies. But just because technology can be used unethically, it does not mean that the entire technology is evil. It just means that efforts must be made to use it in an ethical way.

Is social media a force for good or evil? There's no clear-cut answer, as social media has clearly been used for both positive and negative purposes. Much of the early discussion about social media talked about it being a positive force. Facebook founder Mark Zuckerberg said in 2012: 'By giving people the power to share, we're making the world more transparent.' The following year, Twitter founder Jack Dorsey said: 'When people come to Twitter and they want to express something in the world, the technology fades away. It's them writing a simple message and them knowing that people are going to see it.'

Like any technology, as social media platforms have grown from niche to mass adoption, there are both evangelists and critics. As it has evolved, social media has become a core part of our international communications infrastructure and information ecosystem.

Social media can be manipulated

Information warfare is nothing new, but Russian government-backed groups and organizations seemed to be far ahead of the game in the 2010s, and mobilized memes for information warfare.[1] Russia's Internet Research Agency (IRA) is a prime example. It had been causing headaches for a long time, and its malicious activities were an open secret. An exposé in the *New York Times* in 2015 said that 'From a nondescript office building in St Petersburg, Russia, an army of well-paid "trolls" has tried to wreak havoc all around the Internet – and in real-life American communities.'[2]

Their online activities can be directly traced back to 2011, when what may have started as pro-Kremlin operations inside Russia expanded worldwide with remarkable speed.

On 11 September 2014, an elaborate and well-organized social media hoax spread panic about a supposed terrorist attack on a chemical plant in Louisiana. Hundreds of Twitter accounts were spreading false news and videos of a chemical plant exploding, including supposed local footage. Journalists, politicians and local influencers were bombarded with news of this supposed attack, with links to other social media sites including video footage on YouTube, doctored photos suggesting the story had been picked up by CNN, and screenshots purporting to be alerts from the chemical plant. Similar patterns of disinformation campaigns were spotted in subsequent years using similar tactics.

The investigation by the *New York Times* found that the Moscow-based IRA were spreading stories, faking comments and attempting to influence news and shape opinions around the world. Much of the activity focused on influencing opinion related to the civil war between Ukraine and Russian-backed separatists that began in 2014, churning out comments and content that were positive about the Kremlin.

While there was initial speculation about Russia's influence on major political events, there is now hard evidence that the IRA spread their own information, memes and fake news related to the US Presidential election in 2016. Oxford University's Computational Propaganda Research Project conducted a comprehensive study, commissioned by the US Congress, of the IRA's influence.[3]

The IRA used fairly standard tactics to spread information on major social media networks like Facebook, Twitter and Instagram. They reached tens of millions of users in the United States, and over 30 million users shared content from IRA-controlled pages. The IRA ran dozens of pages, targeting different demographic and interest groups representing diverse communities from across the United States.

They specifically used different types of pages to target different groups, with group names like 'Being Patriotic' (over 6 million likes), 'Heart of Texas' (over 5 million),

'Blacktivist' (more than 4.5 million) and 'LGBT United' (about 2 million). The research from Oxford showed that they targeted right-leaning groups with pro-Trump advertising, while spreading information to minority and left-leaning groups designed to spread mistrust in institutions, all the time encouraging people not to vote.

As has long been the practice by the IRA, most of the content was not political, but intended to encourage engagement and collect more followers using clickbait, humour and memes. One of the interesting observations about the IRA's tactics is that they are similar in many ways to commercial practices that aim to gain influence on social media and in marketing. That's not to say that what they did was good or right, but these are not hackers – they are a large, efficient and knowledgeable organization taking advantage of the digital infrastructure that is already available.

From information warfare to kinetic warfare

In 2021 and 2022 social media became part of a different type of battleground, with boots and tank treads on the ground. Armed conflict in Ukraine had been ongoing for more than seven years, with more than 14,000[4] people losing their lives by 2021. But for the first seven years, the war had largely been confined to two regions in eastern Ukraine.

In late 2021 Russia began to amass tens of thousands of troops on Ukraine's borders with Russia and Belarus under the guise of 'military exercises'. By November, British ministers were expressing 'significant concern' about a build-up of nearly 100,000 troops on the Ukrainian border. Alongside this, social media was being flooded with images and videos of Russian troops and military equipment moving by rail and road. Open Source Intelligence (OSINT) commentators were sharing information and analysis that was derived completely from information that was available in the public domain. One commentator who goes by @OSINTtechnical on Twitter said in December 2021 that the best warning sign of an imminent Russian invasion would be the movement of aviation assets to forward airbases.[5]

This movement of Russian aircraft happened in subsequent weeks. One report from the Russian Ministry of Defence[6] announced movement of bombers to an airbase 500km away from Ukraine. Reports from open-source aircraft-tracking applications and social media users continued through January 2022. In late January, liveuamap, an online open-source mapping platform, showed that Russian SU25S planes were being redeployed from eastern Russian districts to Belarus.[7]

By mid-January 2022 the bulk of Britain's military transport aircraft were supplying anti-tank weapons to Ukraine.[8] None of this was happening in secret. All this activity was unfolding in real time across social media. It was easy to watch with flight-tracking apps showing the C-17 military transport aircraft moving between the US, UK and Eastern Europe. Videos of ground troops and military hardware moving across Russia towards Ukraine were being uploaded and shared continuously on Twitter and TikTok, as well as other platforms.

Most people have both smartphones and social media so it's nearly impossible to move large amounts of military equipment without local people recording and sharing that evidence online. It's highly likely that ministries and departments of defence in NATO countries were looking at the same information that was being reported by plane spotters, open-source intelligence commentators and the general population on the ground in Russia, Belarus and Ukraine.

This is important, and it affects all social media users, whether they are consumers or marketers, because these platforms are being used to share information and disinformation, to form and shape narratives on global events, including wars. Social media activity isn't independent of these physical battlefields, it becomes part of the battlefields. This dark side of social media (as well as the commentators who were warning about it, and sharing information) is embedded in the platforms we are all using. We can't pretend they don't exist, or that our activities can be independent of other global events. But if we choose to participate in social media platforms, we should be very careful about how we get involved, and what information we choose to like, share or contribute to.

Lessons for social media marketers

Marketing has always been accused of being a type of 'dark art'. Attempting to influence people to buy products, sway opinions and encourage specific behaviours has the potential to draw criticism.

Advertising campaigns about smoking are a prime example: early slick advertisements attempted, quite successfully, to portray inhaling a cocktail of carcinogens as fun, youthful, sexy and healthy. Lucky Strikes were marketed as 'Your throat protection against irritation, against cough' or 'More doctors smoke Camels than any other cigarette' – even 'As your dentist, I would recommend Viceroys' (a brand of cigarettes).

Many of the tactics used by state-backed social media influence campaigns are fairly basic techniques for spreading messages used by many marketing organizations:

- **Create memorable, shareable content** – create content, whether articles, lists, photos, videos or memes, that makes a strong and immediate impression. Content should be on topics that people want to discuss on social media and share with their friends or connections.
- **Create topical content** – content that is current and relevant will generate more user engagement, garner interest and draw people into the discussion.
- **Repurpose popular content** – revise and reuse the most popular content in different ways or on different channels. Repackage and revise 'evergreen' content in diverse ways for diverse audiences.
- **Engage your audience** – get activity and posts that encourage people to like, comment and share. This will attract a larger audience – social media sites will promote and feature content that is generating a great deal of interest.
- **Work with influencers** – collaborating with popular users or channels can get people interested in those connections, the relationships between different influencers and their content.

Companies, organizations and individuals who want to build a positive reputation or interact with groups and communities and individuals on social media should not use dark or destructive methods to achieve their aims. The lesson here is that eventually the truth will be found out. This type of unethical activity would be incredibly damaging for any company operating in a democratic country.

Below are some guidelines to help you ensure you are using social media in an ethical way.

Ethical guidelines: a defence against the dark arts

To ensure you're not being seen as practising dark arts, we've included ethical guidelines for activities on social media adapted from National Social Marketing Centre guidelines:[9]

- **Avoiding discrimination against certain groups:** do not deliberately exclude certain groups, and avoid using harmful stereotypes or prejudice against these groups.
- **Minimizing potential harm:** be careful when attempting to influence people's beliefs or call them to action. A common example of this on social media is threats or incitements of violence. This type of activity is not just unethical; it is also often illegal.
- **Informed and voluntary consent:** be clear and transparent about what activities you are carrying out, how any data the company collects will be used, and the effects of any user interaction. The General Data Protection Regulation (GDPR) in the EU comprehensively covers your responsibilities.

- **Respect for privacy and confidentiality**: this is closely tied to informed and voluntary consent. People who engage with an organization's social media must be clearly informed about what data they are sharing and how it will be used. When organizations engage in activities such as handling complaints or using customer feedback on social media, privacy and confidentiality must be respected.
- **Honesty and avoiding deception**: any organization using social media as part of their business should be direct and honest about what their activities are and why they are doing it, and should not use social media to lie or misinform. When mistakes happen, there should be a mechanism to clarify or correct.
- **Avoiding (or declaring) conflicts of interest**: this is particularly relevant for marketing content. Influencer accounts often contain a mix of general content and paid content from third parties. Declaring conflicts of interest is simple: be clear and honest about any third parties who have a relationship with the content.

These guidelines can serve as a useful template, but any company with a social media strategy should develop their own policy for social media use. There may be different requirements for different business activities, and most professional associations will have their own advice that must be integrated.

The National Social Marketing Centre provides a useful outline, along with a detailed handbook on developing your own ethical guidelines.

Conclusion

Social media can be used to sell everything from useless products to toxic ideologies. But just because technology can be used unethically or with malicious intent, it does not mean that the entire technology is evil. It just means that efforts must be made to use it in an ethical way. Those using social media should make sure their activities adhere to strong, ethical guidelines.

Notes

1   MacRae, I (2021) *Dark Social: Understanding the darker side of work, personality and social media*, Bloomsbury, London
2   New York Times Magazine (2015) The agency: www.nytimes.com/2015/06/07/magazine/the-agency.html (archived at https://perma.cc/9946-P4CE)
3   Computational propaganda research project (nd) The IRA, social media and political polarization in the United States, 2012–2018: https://comprop.oii.ox.ac.uk/wp-content/uploads/sites/93/2018/12/The-IRA-Social-Media-and-Political-Polarization.pdf (archived at https://perma.cc/V58M-GUJR)
4   BBC News (2021) Russia Ukraine: Putin compares Donbas war zone to genocide: https://www.bbc.com/news/world-europe-59599066 (archived at https://perma.cc/KC2S-ZXQC)
5   Listen Notes (2021) The OSINT Bunker podcast S2E08, 20 December: https://www.listennotes.com/podcasts/the-osint-bunker/the-osint-bunker-s2e08-20th-dH_MhNCZLpG/ (archived at https://perma.cc/H4KZ-G6NW)
6   Ministry of Defence of the Russian Federation (2021) A batch of Su-34 bombers has arrived at Lipetsk Aviation Center of the VKS: https://eng.mil.ru/en/news_page/country/more.htm?id=12400073@egNews (archived at https://perma.cc/5VVR-4GGJ)

7   liveuamap (2022) Su-35S fighter jets from Russian Eastern Military
    District moved to Belarus: https://belarus.liveuamap.com/en/2022/22-
    january-su35s-fighter-jets-from-russian-eastern-military (archived at
    https://perma.cc/5DGM-Z3EQ)

8   UK Defence Journal (2022) British military aircraft rapidly supplying
    weapons to Ukraine: https://ukdefencejournal.org.uk/british-aircraft-
    transporting-anti-armour-weapons-to-ukraine/ (archived at https://
    perma.cc/5TQ6-LJZU)

9   UWE Research Repository (2009) Social marketing ethics: Report prepared
    for the National Social Marketing Centre: http://eprints.uwe.ac.uk/54/1/
    NSMC_Ethics_Report.pdf (archived at https://perma.cc/CZ9M-KBCC)

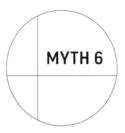

MYTH 6

It's not worth responding to criticism on social media

It can take a bit of work to sort the troublemakers from the legitimate complaints. But responding to complaints and criticism on social media is well worth the effort when it is done well.

Most activity on social media happens publicly. That can be great when things are going well and the tone is positive, but criticism on social media can get out of control when it is ignored or handled poorly. One of the risks for any business active on social media is that negative interactions are publicly visible. Even the most effective businesses sometimes make mistakes, and even the most well-intentioned organizations may come up against people with intentions that are not entirely constructive.

Avoiding social media does not free companies from criticism online. People will take to social media to complain about businesses or products they have a problem with, even if the organization is not on social media. But if you participate in social media, you can respond to these complaints directly and actively manage your reputation online.

Do not assume complaints or criticism are always a problem. Those doing the complaining often have a resolution in mind so problems can be quick and easy to fix. Many people take to social media when they haven't been able to solve their problem in a traditional setting such as in person or on the phone. But as social media is increasingly proving itself to be the quickest way to fix problems, a growing number of people are now using it as their first port of call. If there is a solution to be had, these complaints are a good opportunity for the organization to recognize, address, and solve the problem, which will satisfy most people. Publicly solving someone's problem or fixing a mistake demonstrates how others can expect that person or organization to act in the future.

Of course, not everyone has the best intentions online. A small minority of people do just like to cause chaos and stir up trouble. This means it can take a bit of work to sort the troublemakers from the legitimate complaints. But responding to complaints and criticism on social media is well worth the effort when it is done well.

Response times

Social media is a fast-moving communication platform. For better or worse, many people will be quick to take to social media, sometimes even narrating their problem or complaint in real time. As discussed in Myth 12, your business does not necessarily need to be online 24/7, but you should have target response times for interactions on social media.

Responding quickly and diffusing tensions can help to keep the problem from escalating and shows the person that you are listening and taking them seriously. Pay careful attention to what the person is saying in their first post. If they are asking for something clear and concrete, it should make the response straightforward. Identify their problem, what resolution they are looking for, and whether that outcome is possible. If their product was faulty, there should be some clear steps to rectifying the problem. If they had a poor customer service experience, perhaps an apology is in order. The first thing you should try to identify is what their desired outcome is (or was). Complaints, in general, should be relatively straightforward to resolve in a satisfactory way if you know what the other person wants to get out of the interaction.

If you cannot figure out what the person who is complaining wants to achieve, or they will not tell you, perhaps there is nothing more that can be offered than an apology. For any lengthier interaction, or if a solution is not easily identifiable, it may be better to have the discussion in private or via direct messages instead of a public forum.

Public vs private responses

Not all public complaints require a public response, and public forums are not always the best place to solve complex problems. If a quick and easy fix or a simple apology is all that is required, then a public response may be a good option. If the problem cannot be solved in 280 characters, a private conversation may be a much better approach.

In many cases, people take to social media for a response when they cannot get through to a real person. Some companies deliberately set up convoluted and automated messaging services to make it almost impossible to talk with a real person at the business. Others simply advise callers to check the website shortly before the phone line disconnects.

This often results in frustration, and some people will choose to take to social media after their other options for making a complaint or venting their frustrations are thwarted. Unless your business model involves deliberately blocking people from contacting you, a good solution could be to offer a direct message, email or phone contact to the person who has a complaint.

Complaints on a public forum can sometimes turn into grandstanding. In public confrontations, both sides are more likely to try and save face or be seen as the winner of a conflict, and this can be counterproductive when trying to come to a resolution. It can be easier for both sides to de-escalate conflict, work to solve a complex problem and come to a satisfactory resolution without bystanders and spectators.

Do not escalate

For many people, the natural response to complaints or criticism is to defend. It may relate to an oversight which happened despite the best intentions of people in the company. Or it may be a problem that was completely outside of the organization's control. Maybe the criticism is too aggressively directed at people who genuinely want to help. Sometimes people and organizations are hesitant to admit fault, worrying that it could compound the problem. In most cases, though, an apology and a promise to resolve the issue goes a long way. When possible and reasonable, the apology should offer a remedy to the problem or concrete steps towards a resolution.

Of course, anyone who has worked in customer service (these authors included) know that some people have complaints that the business cannot solve. Some people come in looking for a fight that has nothing to do with their target. A few people have other things going on in their lives and end up making an innocent bystander the target of their own troubled mind. This cannot be avoided, but if there is clearly no resolution to the problem then avoid making the situation worse, de-escalate as much as feasible or reasonable, and quietly allow the person to move along.

If the claims are inaccurate or deliberately mischievous, it may be necessary to correct the information, and provide facts supporting your message. Always be polite. If both sides persist in lowering the tone of the discussion on social media, the whole affair can descend into madness. If you take the bait, it just fuels more activity and may even signal to others that you will engage in behaviour where no one escapes looking good.

Return to the initial point of trying to figure out what people's desired outcomes are when they make complaints online.

Actions follow words

Promises are easy to make, but it's very important that reasonable steps are taken to follow through on what people are told on social media. If the promise is to fix, or investigate, the problem, then those promises must be put into action.

If the issue is complex or will take some time to solve, keep people updated on progress. Even if the problem cannot be solved in a way that will completely satisfy the complainant, they should still see that you have taken all reasonable steps to fix it, or at least to figure out and explain what went wrong.

A quick response and an apology may help in the short term, but it will not help if the necessary action is not taken to address the issue.

Remember your customer base

We've said that it is important to identify people's objectives when they make a complaint on social media, as well as highlighting that a small minority of people just want to cause chaos instead of having constructive intentions.

Always consider your customer or client base when responding to criticism. We've discussed extensively the importance of specific messages, targeting markets and having a clearly defined approach to social media (see Myths 12 and 27). Remember that your general approach to social media and how you interact with people online shouldn't break your focus on your core audience.

A furore can quickly break out on social media and sweep up many in its path. At times, the immediacy of social media can make problems seem far more serious in the moment than they will be with the perspective of hindsight and time. Keep this in mind, take a breath and a pause, put your phone or laptop down for a few moments and re-evaluate your response to flashpoints.

While it is important to apologize for mistakes and acknowledge and resolve legitimate complaints, be more cautious about getting mixed up in a controversy that is not directly related to your organization, its customers or its stakeholders. If a group are unhappy with your organization, but have no relationship with you and are never likely to be customers, then their criticisms can be taken with a very large grain of salt.

It's not possible to make everyone happy on social media, so make sure you don't throw your own customers or employees under the bus to appease virtual pitchfork-wielding mobs.

Employee guidelines

We discuss employee guidelines for social media in Myths 7 and 14. There is no need to restate them in detail, but your guidelines should explain how to interact with complainants on the organization's social media account or when acting on behalf of the organization.

Guidelines for staff who manage social media accounts should also include what types of behaviour on social media are unacceptable. Although much of this myth has focused on customer complaints and resolving customer problems, it is very important to remember the well-being of the public-facing employees who deal with these complaints. While legitimate criticisms and genuine complaints may not always be expressed in the most civilized manner, abuse, harassment or discrimination against staff must not be tolerated.

Conclusion

It is worth responding to criticism on social media. If you communicate with people in a respectful way that aligns with your overall communications style and strategy, it can be an opportunity to improve the overall customer experience and relationships.

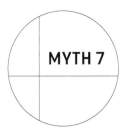

MYTH 7

Sharing more content is always better

If you want to saturate people with low-cost and high-frequency content, social media will certainly support that. But it is not the best way to get people's attention or admiration for your brand.

If you look for guidelines for posting on social media, you will find all sorts of suggestions and recommendations: how much to share, how often, what times of day and what kinds of images, video, infographics and other media can be useful to get your message across. These can be very helpful, but remember, these are guidelines – not absolute rules.

Generally, Monday through to Friday during regular working hours are the most active times on social media. Friday and Saturday evenings often have lower activity, and the fewest people are online in the middle of the night (about 10 pm to 4 am). But if your business promotes something related to nightlife, Friday and Saturday evenings might be better. If you are selling hangover cures, Saturday and Sunday mornings might be the best times to advertise your products.

While oversharing or over-saturating users with content is not ideal, being inactive is just as bad. Any business that started a social media profile a decade ago, posted a few dozen times in that period and has been inactive for the past few years should be embarrassed. It's better not to have a social media profile than to have one that is clearly neglected.

Let's start with oversharing. Oversharing can mean either posting too frequently, or sharing details that are far more personal than strangers on the internet want to hear. It can be a minor inconvenience to readers, but some people take it to the level of a digital plague, splurging so much incomprehensible or unnecessary information that it blots out the intended message and just becomes spam.

Getting too personal

Oversharers are great from the perspective of a hiring manager who likes to act as a digital detective. If someone puts intimate details of their personal and work life online for all to see, that information may be seen as fair game when it comes to making hiring decisions.

If someone has a long history of being openly and publicly belligerent, of initiating and escalating arguments and being consistently aggressive (or passive-aggressive) towards friends and/or strangers, that may be a good indication of their likely future behaviour in the workplace. If people display serious problems with judgement and impulse control on social media, a hiring manager may justifiably decide that their actions would not be desirable in the office.

We discuss what kind of information is fair game in Myths 21 and 29, but the rule of thumb is that if someone makes their own information publicly available, other people are likely to see it. Whether or not employers are allowed to access this information and consequently make employment decisions based on it is another matter, depending on the country, local employment and data protection regulations, as well as the nature of the work.[1,2]

Social media can be a double-edged sword. According to a Harris Poll, 54 per cent of recruiters say they have decided not to hire a job candidate because of information they saw on the candidate's social media profiles.[3] However, too little can be just as bad as not enough. Over half (57 per cent) also said they are less likely to interview a candidate who they could not find online, and 44 per cent said they found information on social media that made the candidate a more desirable hire.

When people choose to share their own personal information, the outcomes are their responsibility. But what about when people decide to overshare a company's or customer's information? That way leads to danger.

Loose lips sink ships

How often do employees share private or confidential company information on social media? All the time. It's worse than a bit of office gossip or loose lips at the pub, because once it's posted on social media, it's very difficult or impossible to delete. There was an instructive and amusing case in 2013, when struggling UK music retailer HMV went through a large process of layoffs. Thanks to Twitter and screenshots, the social media saga of a disgruntled employee live-tweeting the entire process is still visible to this day.[4]

The tweets began at about 9 am, describing the layoffs process in lurid detail from the inside: 'We're tweeting live from HR where we're all being fired! Exciting!!' They went on: 'Under usual circumstances, we'd never dare to do such a thing as this. However, when the company you dearly love is being ruined…'

The very public and very trending tweets went on to detail how angry the people being fired were, as well as going into detail about the process and those involved. 'Just overheard our Marketing Director (he's staying folks) ask "How do I shut down Twitter?"'

The tweets continued on and off throughout the day, with various details emerging, apparently in a struggle for control over the corporate Twitter account between those employees remaining with the company and those being laid off. Most of the posts were deleted from Twitter, but the records will remain on the internet, with the final tweet of the saga reading: 'There have been job losses today, but not in our stores. We are still open for business, thx for your continued support #savehmv'. Save HMV, indeed. Not great PR for an already-floundering business.

It is easy to make mistakes, though, and sometimes smart and well-meaning people make gaffes on social media. In

2014 Twitter's CFO accidentally published some very sensitive details about a company acquisition publicly instead of in a private message: 'I still think we should buy them. He is on your schedule for Dec 15 or 16 – we will need to sell him.'[5] Although these kinds of mistakes are easy to make, they can have significant consequences.

It is therefore essential to have a sensible policy and clear practice guidelines for social media use in the workplace. The UK General Data Protection Regulation (GDPR) is identical to data protection regulations across the European Union, which makes this even more important for businesses. It has specific requirements for recording, accessing and secure storage and access of data. We'll discuss this in greater detail in Myth 29.

THE GENERAL DATA PROTECTION REGULATION (GDPR)

In the UK and Europe, all companies are required to meet certain regulatory requirements if they process and handle data. This means there are strict rules, and if a company or employee shares someone's personal data or information on social media, the company would fall foul of the data protection regulation. Here are some quick facts about GDPR:

Any data about individuals held by a business (including customers and employees) is considered 'personal data'.

Companies are responsible for any breaches or problems affecting that data. This includes if it is lost or damaged, hacked, stolen or otherwise compromised (including being shared without consent on social media).

Generally, people must consent to having their data collected, and be informed about how it will be used.

Anyone is allowed to access the data that a company stores about them. This includes what type of data, the exact data, where it has been used and who it has been shared with. Any sharing or posting of someone's personal data on social media will raise some awkward questions (as well as being a legal violation).

In the case of breaches of GDPR, companies can be fined up to €10 million or 2 per cent of the firm's global turnover (whichever is the greater).

Since GDPR has come into force, over €1 billion in fines has been issued for data protection violations across Europe, with most fines being levied against Amazon, Google and companies owned by Meta (formerly Facebook).[6]

Brands oversharing

Companies can also overshare on social media. It's great to be active, to connect directly with customers and be responsive on social media. But it's best not to bog people down with an incessant stream of fatuous content.

It's important that companies be educated and savvy consumers and users of social media, and avoid taking some of the bad habits of the past online. If you want to saturate people with low-cost and high-frequency content, social media will certainly support that. But it is not the best way to get people's attention or admiration for your brand.

Post-happy social media managers

Below are some problems that can occur when social media managers are careless and too quick to post:

- **Sharing from the wrong account.** Many social media managers have multiple social accounts. Maybe a company's social media manager volunteers their skills to manage the social profiles of a charity. Perhaps they have their own personal page, pages for their pets, projects or political views. Then, if they are a bit too quick to post, they end up posting the wrong thing to the wrong account. Easy to do – but the consequences can vary from minor to severe.

- **Mixing up direct messages and public posts.** This happens all the time too, like the example from the CFO of Twitter accidentally hinting at a company acquisition in a public post instead of a direct message. It's a very easy mistake to make. Company social media accounts need to be clearly separated from other accounts.

- **Sharing your search queries.** Ever post something on social media that you meant to search for? Instead of typing it in to the search box and hitting Enter, your query ends up posted publicly for everyone to see. April 28 in the UK celebrates and commemorates this mistake, with annual Ed Balls Day festivities, #edballsday

- **Sharing your location.** Most social media platforms have a location-based feature which allows you to tag yourself in a certain geographic location. Many also automatically share this location (unless disabled). Generally, it's a rather benign and slightly interesting feature, but there are times when a person's location can give away a great deal of information. In the same way the Twitter CFO's accidental tweet gave away information about a potential acquisition, a person's location could give a similar hint.

Oversharing is not always about deliberately sharing too much. However, social media companies are set up to collect and share a great deal of data – and that data can sometimes reveal information that a company or their social media manager may not wish to make publicly known.

Conclusion

Sharing more content is not always better. Just because you can put anything out into cyberspace doesn't mean you should. Making mistakes in digital spaces can come with real-world consequences.

Notes

1 Can your social media profile kill your job prospects? www.bbc.co.uk/news/business-42621920 (archived at https://perma.cc/HSV3-DBWN)
2 The GDPR and its effect on social media screening: https://checkpoint.cvcheck.com/the-gdpr-and-its-effect-on-social-media-screening/ (archived at https://perma.cc/CC7Z-J5ST)
3 Number of employers using social media to screen candidates at all-time high, finds latest CareerBuilder study: http://press.careerbuilder.com/2017-06-15-Number-of-Employers-Using-Social-Media-to-Screen-Candidates-at-All-Time-High-Finds-Latest-CareerBuilder-Study (archived at https://perma.cc/R7V8-3V2S)

4   HMV employees go on Twitter rampage while being fired: http://nymag.
    com/intelligencer/2013/01/hmv-twitter-fired-social-media.html (archived
    at https://perma.cc/82QX-Q9Q7)

5   Twitter executive mistakenly tweets about M&A plans: www.telegraph.
    co.uk/finance/newsbysector/mediatechnologyandtelecoms/11252260/
    Twitter-executive-mistakenly-tweets-about-MandA-plans.html (archived
    at https://perma.cc/Z6U7-PF3Q)

6   GDPR fines in Q3 almost hit €1 billion, 20x more than in Q1 and Q2
    combined: https://finbold.com/gdpr-fines-q3-2021/ (archived at https://
    perma.cc/6TT8-Q8BM)

MYTH 8

Social media is free

From a practical perspective, the time and complex resources required to effectively manage the many facets of being 'social' make social media activity anything but free.

When putting this myth into the mix, we questioned ourselves. Given how widely social media has now been embraced within business, and the dominance of activated paid campaigns, do people really still think of the platforms as 'free'?

One of the key fundamentals of any successful social networking site is a strong user base. Significant volumes of users are necessary to make the concept work – after all, not much socializing or networking happens in an empty room.

The heritage of social networks being free to join clearly helped drive significant user numbers. No joining fees made adoption simple and friction-free, as well as easy for those on the platforms to invite others to join in too.

However, the fact that global mainstream social networks such as Twitter, Facebook, Instagram, LinkedIn, Snapchat and messenger services such as WhatsApp and WeChat (to name just a few) are free to access has historically held back adoption of these communication channels within businesses. Think of the age-old adage: if something is free, people tend not to value it highly. Add to this other challenges and concerns such as data ownership and lack of proprietary platform control, which can make social media channels a risky and unattractive proposition in a commercial setting. The risk is vividly brought to life by this analogy from Scott DeLong, the founder of ViralNova, a start-up business built around Facebook: 'Building a start-up dependent on Facebook is like opening a McDonald's on an active volcano.'[1]

This myth explores how the lack of any charges for using social networks has potentially impacted the recognition of their significance among businesses. We also look at how, while the many channels may be fee-free, there are in fact several associated costs. From a practical perspective, the time and complex resources required to effectively manage the many facets of being 'social' make social media activity anything but free.

When free isn't really free

There are millions of businesses boasting that Facebook's platform has enabled them to grow and develop in a way that, had the platform not existed, would not have been possible.

Indeed, Deloitte details how Facebook has stimulated economic growth through three broad effects:[2]

1 as a tool for marketers big and small;
2 as a platform for app development;
3 as a catalyst for connectivity.

The report estimates that through these three channels, Facebook enabled £176 billion of economic impact and 4.5 million jobs globally in 2014 – excluding the operations of the company itself.

With that sort of impact, and knowing that both start-up businesses and established ones depend on it, it begs the question: if there's real business value in the use of the platform, then why not charge subscription fees?

One reason may be the competitive landscape. If all social media networks are free, then it sets a precedent for all platforms to fall in line. No one wants to break rank and lose followers to platforms where networking and sharing content is free. However, the main reason is likely to be how these 'forever-free' platforms drive revenue. This brings us back to the size and strength of their user bases, and the opportunity the data creates for businesses and brands to target and advertise to relevant audiences.

It's estimated that Twitter generates approximately £2.4 billion per annum from advertising.[3] LinkedIn brings in around £2.2 billion annually[4] and the Facebook family, rebranded in 2021 as Meta, including Instagram and WhatsApp, tops the table at a whopping £84.6 billion per year.[5]

Advertising is big business for the social networks. Their survival depends on those strong user bases, and the millions, or billions, of people sharing their valuable personal data – continuously evolving their digital footprint as they go about their daily lives.

While consumers are becoming increasingly sensitive to their personal data being exploited – a concern that's exacerbated by highly visible data scandals such as the Cambridge Analytica case (in which it was reported that Facebook lost £29 billion overnight) – what this means for network advertising revenue is yet to be seen. Currently, there's no evidence of any mass exodus from any of the popular social networking platforms.[6,7]

Beyond targeting social users with adverts, data is also used by brands and organizations to build demographic insights which can be applied to other forms of advertising and product innovation and development. The free use of the social media networks for our data exchange certainly provides more than enough value to keep the networks forever free.

Insight and management – for a fee

Social listening, as we will discuss in Myth 27, is now big business – and over the past decade a new industry has developed. Leading social media monitoring organizations such as Brandwatch and Meltwater (and again, there are many) deliver real-time digital consumer intelligence, driven by the continuous conversations, trends and data signals happening across social networks.

Such real-world, real-time intelligence enables businesses to better manage and optimize campaign performance, become more effective and agile in their marketing activity, spot opportunities and innovate new products. A case study by Danone[8] describes how they listened to relevant comments across social media channels, resulting in the insight that many consumers were seeking lactose-free choices. This resulted in the production of Activia's lactose-free yoghurt.

There are several ways businesses can carry out basic social listening, using free tools such as Google Alerts, but such resources don't come close to the sophisticated enterprise-level resources on offer. Of course, such insights come at a cost – with fees varying depending on functionality and features required.

For businesses active on multiple social networks, there are now hundreds of freemium and enterprise-level resources available to help brands and organizations manage a portfolio of accounts. Social media management platforms such as Hootsuite, Sprout Social, Falcon, Buffer and Salesforce enable social media accounts to be managed via a central dashboard, streamlining content sharing and scheduling of content and engagement. In most cases, these platforms provide social listening too. While some management platforms have a free starter offering, the majority are subscription fees based – varying from a few pounds to a few thousand pounds per month.

The social media service industry

Social media activity is now firmly part of most organizations' digital strategy. In line with this, digital marketing and traditional PR agencies have extended their services to include social media – and a whole new industry of specialist social media agencies has evolved. Just as with any agency, the range of services offered and fees charged varies dependent upon the scale and size of the project in hand. It's highly unlikely that any agency will be working for free!

While it's difficult to determine an estimated value for the social media industry as a whole, Statista suggests:

- revenue in social media advertising segments is projected to reach £122 billion in 2022;
- revenue is expected to show an annual growth rate of 8.7 per cent, resulting in market volume of £170 billion by 2026.[9]

Advertising is a key component of social media revenue; however, so too are there likely to be significant revenues generated by organizations that have become part of the social media service industry, delivering and supporting related activities such as video content development, content development, content marketing, organic social media management, paid social media advertising, social listening, sentiment analysis, channel analytics and data insights – and the list could go on.

The cost of time

While we've considered the costs related to advertising, outsourcing and procuring professional solutions relating to social media activity, there are also the very real costs associated with your time. If you're outsourcing the service, it will still take time to manage partners and agencies – and if you're managing social media activity internally, there's the time required to develop and manage internal competence, staffing, training and associated resources such as content development.

Misunderstood at board level

While social media has evolved into a global commercial industry enabling organizations to engage directly with external customers, relevant influencers and bring about online connection with their own employees, organizations often still underestimate the reach and influence of social media. The heritage of these channels being 'free', and the continued misconception that the platforms are largely filled with inane noise and people still sharing pictures of their lunch, has potentially hampered the adoption of social media strategy by organizational leaders.

During the Covid-19 pandemic, digital adoption took a quantum leap, significantly transforming the digital business landscape forever.[10] Social media platforms, both internal and external, became even more prevalent. Yet, within many boardrooms, when it comes to the role of social media, there is still confusion. The belief that the 'social-savvy' apprentice can manage the social media activity for a brand or organization, without any formal marketing and communication training or strategic business understanding, has led to a number of social media brand blunders and reputational crises, many of which have been well documented in the press. You can read about some of these in *Great Brand Blunders* by Rob Gray.[11]

Had social media channels never been free to use, with significant financial investment around procurement and implementation of the platforms (as is the case with global internal communication CRM systems or cloud operating systems), then it is likely more rigour would have gone into investigating performance and deliverables by those making important financial decisions in the boardroom.

This leads us to another component of the social media industry: education and training. While we can't find a specific number related to global revenue generated associated with social media training, when searching Google, the term 'social media training' returns a whopping 5,290,000,000 results. A growing number of organizations are making social media training compulsory within their organizations and leadership teams, for example Lego enforcing social media exams.[12]

Training, as with so many other aspects associated with social media as outlined in this myth, comes at a cost.

Conclusion

It's likely that social media channels will continue to be free of charge to use, because the data that is generated delivers significant value. But using the channels effectively brings very real associated costs, so should be aligned to your business strategy.

Notes

1   Building a startup on the back of Facebook is like 'opening a McDonald's on an active volcano': www.businessinsider.com/startups-that-rely-on-facebook-2014-1?r=US&IR=T (archived at https://perma.cc/4HLE-6WWF)

2   Facebook's global economic impact: A report for Facebook: www2.deloitte.com/content/dam/Deloitte/uk/Documents/technology-media-telecommunications/deloitte-uk-global-economic-impact-of-facebook.pdf (archived at https://perma.cc/AJB8-2YUC)

3   Annual revenue of Twitter from 2010 to 2020, by segment: https://www.statista.com/statistics/274566/twitters-annual-revenue-by-channel/ (archived at https://perma.cc/CFH3-PNRD)

4   Microsoft says LinkedIn topped $3 billion in ad revenue in the last year, outpacing Snap and Pinterest: www.cnbc.com/2021/04/27/microsoft-linkedin-topped-3-billion-in-ad-revenue-in-last-year.html (archived at https://perma.cc/S3BP-UT2C)

5   Meta's (formerly Facebook Inc) advertising revenue worldwide from 2009 to 2021: https://www.statista.com/statistics/271258/facebooks-advertising-revenue-worldwide/ (archived at https://perma.cc/V2BH-CSLB)

6   The WIRED guide to your personal data (and who is using it): www.wired.com/story/wired-guide-personal-data-collection/ (archived at https://perma.cc/6EGP-KW5U)

7   Facebook lost $37bn overnight due to Cambridge Analytica data scandal: www.campaignlive.co.uk/article/facebook-lost-37bn-overnight-due-cambridge-analytica-data-scandal/1459876 (archived at https://perma.cc/F4FL-HYJS)

8   How social listening changed what's in your breakfast bowl: https://www.danone.com/stories/articles-list/social-listening-and-the-rise-of-custom-breakfast.html (archived at https://perma.cc/CMQ3-HY2A)

9   Social media advertising market statistics: www.statista.com/outlook/dmo/digital-advertising/social-media-advertising/worldwide?currency=GBP (archived at https://perma.cc/3KTL-2TQJ)

10 How COVID-19 has pushed companies over the technology tipping point – and transformed business forever: www.mckinsey.com/business-functions/strategy-and-corporate-finance/our-insights/how-covid-19-has-pushed-companies-over-the-technology-tipping-point-and-transformed-business-forever (archived at https://perma.cc/5NVQ-BCY2)

11 Gray, R (2014) *Great Brand Blunders*, Crimson Publishing, London

12 Social Brands: Lego forces management to sit social media exams: www.campaignlive.co.uk/article/social-brands-lego-forces-management-sit-social-media-exams/1170028?src_site=brandrepublic (archived at https://perma.cc/F6YR-55MZ)

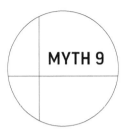

MYTH 9

Social media can replace your business website

Businesses will find social media to be most useful when their marketing and other activities revolve around a clear strategy and central platform.

Some people run very successful businesses entirely on social media. Indeed, a handful of people and certain organizations operate solely this way – but they are the exception rather than the rule. Social media influencers are examples of successful enterprises operating only on social media, and in some cases only on a single channel, attracting large numbers of followers with appealing text or image-based content and then promoting products to them.

Social media websites are advertising platforms, and provide the opportunity to connect with large numbers of users. They typically operate with a very specific and limited type of content. These platforms and their large audiences can be incredibly useful for businesses – but in most cases are not, and should not be, the only place where a business operates.

Reaching your audiences

Social media is an extremely valuable tool for industry, and is often used for promoting businesses or products (as discussed in Myths 10 and 26). It can also be used for internal communications (Myth 13) and for attracting and recruiting employees, and can supplement a range of other business activities and functions. The potential value of social media to business is difficult to overstate – but it is also necessary to acknowledge some of the limitations.

Social media can be very useful for tapping into the large audiences that already exist on different platforms, and connecting with groups that are already active. Some businesses already use social media as a primary channel for operating – for example, estimates suggest at least half of complaining customers take their concerns to social media.[1] Many customers know that certain companies are so focused on social strategies that the business will be more responsive on their social media than through traditional communication channels.

As with any useful tool, it may be tempting to use only that tool. Social media is typically user-friendly and free to use (however, see Myth 8 to understand why social media isn't free). This means that barriers to using it are extremely low, with the potential benefits being significant. But social media must be thought of as a supplement to, not a replacement for, the traditional business website and other business tools.

Supplementary, not a replacement

Social platforms are useful for targeting specific audiences for specific purposes. Twitter, for example, is great for time- and location-specific content. LinkedIn is more suited to discussions of businesses, workplaces and activities such as recruitment. YouTube provides a platform to share video content with over a billion active users.

Social media companies offer different communications platforms, each with their own unique context, norms and culture (as outlined in Myth 2). They may offer some level of customization for users, but are generally quite limited in their available features and functionality compared to a traditional business website.

This can be an advantage when business activities on social media are well-designed and integrated into overall business strategy. However, social media can be far less effective when a scattergun approach is used. It may be tempting to create a business page on every social media channel, then just wait to see what happens.

However, businesses will find social media to be most useful when their marketing and other activities revolve around a clear strategy and central platform. This could be anything from their own website to a physical location. The focus of social channels is to expand their own user base, so the value of a traditional business website remains as high as ever.

Social media is useful for connecting with potential customers or employees, but many of the most successful businesses use these channels simply to direct people to their products or services on their own site. While the traditional business website may be costly to develop and maintain, it offers far greater customization opportunities.

Some companies do operate primarily on social media, or use it for specific functions. Small businesses can use social media to reduce costs, minimize investment in their own resources and take advantage of the tools on offer. However, it is not a good idea to become over-reliant on social media.

The risks of relying on a third party

While social media can be invaluable, it is important to keep in mind that relying on it can be a risky strategy. Remember that social media companies are not benevolent behemoths. They set non-negotiable terms of use which can, and often do, change substantially.

Social platforms benefit from your customers

Social media companies offer their services for free because of the rewards they get from their users. There are significant advantages for businesses in moving customers or clients away from social media to their owned channels.

It's easier to think of this using a physical example. If your owned channel is a physical shop where you sell a product, your ultimate goal is to get people through the doors of that shop and buy from you directly. Getting them to that physical location is a necessary first step. It's great if everyone is talking about your shop on social media, but it's not very effective if that traffic doesn't move into the physical space of the shop. If people are talking about your business on Facebook, those are Facebook's customers. They become your customers once you get them into your shop.

It is the same when an owned channel is online. The business's owned space needs to be the focus of any activity on social media. Encourage people to move between channels and through to your owned channel. Social media may be a good shop window, but it needs to get people through the digital door to be effective.

For many businesses, a list of contacts is an extraordinarily valuable resource – these can be business contacts, potential employees, or current and potential customers. Publications, media and resources are also valuable intellectual property, and the online interactions between businesses and their customers can be a goldmine of information. There is significant value in keeping much of this on your owned channels. This is important for the long-term success and viability of any business, so it is always useful to consider the advantages and disadvantages of publishing your information on social media channels compared with your owned channels.

It's important to remember that the majority of the rewards from your work on social media go to the social media company. For all the interest and online interaction you generate through content, a lot of the benefit goes to that platform. They are more than happy to share their platform with you, so that you can help them obtain user data and advertising revenue. Many businesses and organizations are happy to make this trade-off, but it should be part of a carefully considered strategy.

Social platforms come and go

Some social media consultants live at the mercy of another company's algorithms. They work to generate content that will be picked up by the algorithms of a search engine or social media channel. This is a tactic that may work in the short term, but when the algorithms change, they are left out in the cold.[2]

Social media trends, channels and companies come and go, so businesses must be cautious of depending too much on any particular channel. A business which invests all its time or resources on one social network is putting all its eggs in one basket – and the basket belongs to someone else. The future of that business relies on a single external party.

For a business that has the time and resources, it can be incredibly useful to invest in a variety of social channels that fit with its business. This is most effective when the most appropriate channels are used in conjunction with a company's owned channels. Diversification is an important safety and sustainability mechanism for almost all business activity, and it's the same for social media. If your business only had one customer, who is 95 years old, it would be seriously advisable to diversify your customer base.

What if your main social media channel were to shut down overnight and all your work was deleted? This happens surprisingly frequently. It may feel unlikely, but it is possible: Vine and Friendster are recent now-defunct social media channels. Tech giant Google alone has had its share of social media sites that have flopped, such as Orkut, Dodgeball, Jaiku, Wave, Buzz and Google+.[3]

What happened to the brands or influencers who became popular exclusively on these platforms after they were shut down? If they hadn't built up their owned channels, they would have had to start from square one. Millions of likes, followers or potential customers can disappear just as quickly as they appear.

Conclusion

Social media is most effective when it is used in conjunction with owned channels. It is not a substitute for traditional resources like a business website. Analyse each social and owned channel and consider how to use them in a complementary way.

Notes

1   The Sprout Social Index, Edition XII: Call-out culture: https://sproutsocial.com/insights/data/q3-2017 (archived at https://perma.cc/2EFH-GVSC)
2   Instagram suddenly chokes off developers as Facebook chases privacy: https://techcrunch.com/2018/04/02/instagram-api-limit (archived at https://perma.cc/BD4H-V9HU)
3   A brief history of Google's social networking flops: http://techland.time.com/2011/07/11/a-brief-history-of-googles-social-networking-flops (archived at https://perma.cc/3APV-VZHK)

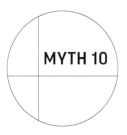

MYTH 10

Social media activity is purely a marketing function

Social media activity is a two-way, one-to-many and many-to-many communication resource, and presents a rich pot of insight from which numerous business units can draw.

Heralded from the outset in the business community as a new and potentially far-reaching channel to market, it was no surprise that social media was initially always managed within marketing departments. Social media directors, managers, executives, consultants and gurus didn't exist. Neither did social media agencies, and there was no such thing as a 'social media strategy' or social media advertising.

Over the same timeframe, digital technology has continued to advance at a blistering rate, with social media engagement further facilitated by the ferocious adoption of the smartphone and associated mobile technology.

Depending upon the size and structure of an organization, it's still not unusual for social media management to sit within the marketing division. There's a natural fit with many aspects of marketing: brand awareness, customer acquisition, customer loyalty, promotions, creative content and audience engagement – both organically and via paid advertising and sponsorship.

However, as we will also touch on in Myth 27, far from swimming in its own lane, social media and its variety of applications is widely relevant for many organizational departments. It is, or should be, enmeshed within customer service, HR, PR, product development, IT, legal, R&D, sales, business development, PR and corporate communications.

In this myth, we'll look at how social media makes an impact outside the marketing sphere.

External-facing social activity

Customer service

As always-on, digitally connected consumers, our customer service expectations have risen in line with technological advances. We expect to be able to contact a business at pretty much any time of day, via our channel of preference – and, importantly, we expect a speedy response.

If things are not going our way, whether it's the fact that our train is delayed, the service we receive is poor or even just slow, or our expectations are dashed by shoddy quality or misrepresentation, then hell hath no fury like our fast fingers on a smartphone keypad.

And of course, social media is not purely used for complaining. When it comes to customer service, we are using social media to ask questions and receive answers and advice.

Research on customer service usage of social networks identified that:[1]

- one in three social media users prefer social media customer care services to telephone or email;
- an estimated 67 per cent of consumers now use social media networks to seek resolution for issues;
- customers spend 20–40 per cent more with companies that engage and respond to customers via social media;
- nearly 70 per cent of consumers have said that they have used social media for issues to do with customer service on at least one occasion.

There are many case studies showing effective use of social media for customer service. The article 'Social customer service: Lessons from 5 of our favorite brands' includes case studies from Nike, Spotify, Skyscanner, Netflix and Starbucks.[2]

Customer service teams are embracing the latest technologies evolving from social platforms, taking advantage of artificial intelligence to segment and speed up customer response times. Thus, many customer service conversations are moving into messenger services such as WhatsApp and Facebook Messenger.

Human resources

For HR teams, social channels have become a staple tool for recruitment and the communication of employer brand.

Social media gives HR teams the opportunity to reach a far larger number of prospective employees at relatively low cost, on a continuous basis. For example, HR teams can communicate organizational culture to attract prospective employees. They can showcase employer brand, share stories and case studies from happy employees, introduce leaders and give an overview of workplace features and benefits.

HR teams can also leverage staff's personal networks by setting up employee referral schemes. Employee referrals have the highest applicant-to-hire conversion rate, accounting for 40 per cent of all hires.[3] Clearly, a strong talent acquisition tactic encourages employees to share hiring opportunities with their networks on social media.

Social media can also help HR teams mitigate costs and brand reputation associated with making the wrong hire. A Career Builder Survey found that 70 per cent of employers use social media to screen candidates during the hiring process.[4] That's a relatively high percentage of employers relying on the collective use of social media to inform their decisions.

Research and development

When it comes to market research, given that over 4 billion people around the world are active on social media for an average of two to three hours a day,[5] and the fact that they tend to share a lot of information about themselves online, there is a significant pot of data from which to collect rich insights.

For example, when GE Life Sciences wanted to learn how customers discussed protein purification, they analysed

500,000 protein-related comments on social media. The data improved their content creation, enabling them to tailor their website in a way which was more aligned with the voice of the customer, and optimize their search strategy.[6]

Referred to by Curt Bloom, then-President of Crimson Hexagon, as 'the biggest focus group on the planet', social media can also assist with getting direct feedback about products, services, new features and beta tests – enabling brands and organizations to optimize in line with the wisdom of the crowd.

Whether it's polls, social listening or interpreting reams of data to analyse audience sentiment, social media has become an important resource in the field of research and development.

Sales

Networking has always played a valuable role for business development and sales professionals. Social networks have become equally valuable, enabling a far wider array of connections and the ability to tune in to what's happening on the ground with prospects and customers.

'Social selling' is the process of sales professionals using social media to find and engage with new prospects. It's effectively the same practice of building rapport and relationships with your prospects in real life – so that when they are ready to buy, you're naturally front of mind.

With social technologies, sales professionals can share relevant content, answer questions, respond and continuously engage from the start of the purchase funnel all the way through to consideration, building rapport and closing the deal.

Internal-facing social activity

In the same way as external-facing social media activity provides opportunities to listen to audiences, engage and connect with customers, prospects and influencers, share marketing messages and keep audiences up to speed with company notices and PR, these valuable activities can also be harnessed and used for internal audiences.

Research shows that 82 per cent of employees believe that social media improves work relationships, and 60 per cent believe social media supports decision-making processes.[7] It has the potential to ease collaboration, make employees feel more involved and connected to their employers, and aid retention.

The Covid-19 pandemic led to a dramatic increase in social media usage around the world.[8] While some organizations already used social networks for internal communication, many accelerated their digital transformation programmes to remain engaged with employees working remotely. Research from Brunswick cites 88 per cent of employees leaning in to social networks to connect and communicate.[9]

Customer service

As mentioned, it's common for the customer service team to have a front-line presence on social media, managing day-to-day conversations and queries with the customer. Such engagement will drive useful insights, which the customer service team can feed back into the business to help drive continuous improvement.

HR

According to the Career Builder Survey mentioned earlier, around 43 per cent of employers use social media to nurture and connect with current employees.

There are some frightening statistics about the level of employee disengagement – with Gallup's State of the Global Workplace Report suggesting that a whopping 85 per cent of employees are either unengaged or actively disengaged at work. The economic consequences of this are approximately £5.4 trillion in lost productivity.[10]

A growing number of case studies demonstrate the positive impact of social media being used internally to regenerate employee engagement (as discussed in Myth 13).

Communications/internal marketing

Social media extends the same benefits it offers externally to internal marketing and communications. Businesses increasingly recognize that keeping their workforce (that is, their internal customers) happy and engaged is just as important as keeping external customers happy. Internal use of social media opens new channels for innovation, dialogue and insight and is fundamental to productivity and business performance. A study by McKinsey Global Institute highlighted the connection between engagement and productivity. It discovered that if companies were to fully implement social media activity internally, they could improve employee productivity by 20 to 25 per cent.[11]

Strategy/leadership

Many of the research articles that we've mentioned describe the role that leaders play in driving organizational connectivity, by staying visible and communicating effectively with employees.

As we explore in Myth 22, a growing swathe of CEOs are taking to the external-facing social media stage – speaking out to keep investors, the media and customers aware of important company updates or viewpoints. However, from an internal perspective, social media technologies enable all leaders, at every level within an organization, to connect and communicate openly and directly with the teams they lead.

Communication is not a one-way street; social media channels offer the opportunity for leaders to listen directly to what employees are saying and, where relevant and appropriate, to respond directly.

Employee advocacy programmes achieve the most success when they have leadership buy-in. Not only is getting leadership involved good for business, but there's opportunity to build the all-important trust factor. Brunswick research found that 88 per cent of respondents felt a leader being active on social media made them more trustworthy.[12]

Conclusion

Social media activity is a two-way, one-to-many and many-to-many communication resource and presents a rich pot of insight from which numerous business units can draw. It is not purely a marketing function; social media activity transcends the confines of any one department.

Notes

1 Social media customer service statistics and trends: www.socialmediatoday.com/social-business/social-media-customer-service-statistics-and-trends-infographic (archived at https://perma.cc/E5CZ-KBXK)

2 Social customer service: Lessons from 5 of our favorite brands: https://mention.com/en/blog/social-customer-service/ (archived at https://perma.cc/4NRT-DNR8)

3 Why employee referrals are the best source of hire: https://theundercoverrecruiter.com/infographic-employee-referrals-hire (archived at https://perma.cc/B2TH-PF5C)

4 Keep it clean: Social media screenings gain in popularity: www.businessnewsdaily.com/2377-social-media-hiring.html (archived at https://perma.cc/R9W4-UAH4)

5 Social media users pass the 4.5 billion mark: https://wearesocial.com/uk/blog/2021/10/social-media-users-pass-the-4-5-billion-mark/ (archived at https://perma.cc/U68D-TLYX)

6 How to use social media for market research: https://conversionxl.com/blog/social-media-market-research (archived at https://perma.cc/6XLS-VT8K)

7 Employees who use social media for work are more engaged – but also more likely to leave their jobs: https://hbr.org/2018/05/employees-who-use-social-media-for-work-are-more-engaged-but-also-more-likely-to-leave-their-jobs (archived at https://perma.cc/6X5T-EMBX)

8 How the pandemic changed social media: https://blog.hubspot.com/marketing/quarantine-trends-social-media (archived at https://perma.cc/8BVP-DDNN)

9 2021 Connected Leadership: https://www.brunswickgroup.com/media/8059/connected-leadership-2021-report.pdf (archived at https://perma.cc/PRD5-A6QB)

10 State of the global workforce report: www.gallup.com/workplace/349484/state-of-the-global-workplace-2022-report.aspx (archived at https://perma.cc/TF7C-DTME)

11 7 reasons social media in the workplace can help employees: https://theolsongroup.com/5-reasons-social-media-workplace-can-help-employees (archived at https://perma.cc/TX8U-UUEX)

12 2021 Connected Leadership: https://www.brunswickgroup.com/media/8059/connected-leadership-2021-report.pdf (archived at https://perma.cc/PRD5-A6QB)

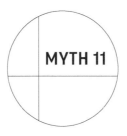

MYTH 11

Social media cannot be done well in-house

As activity on social channels has become more important for businesses, so too has expertise in how to effectively use the channels.

As social media has become mainstream, organizations have invested not only in setting up accounts and profiles, but also in the human capital necessary to manage social media activities such as content and creative campaign development, social listening, social data analytics and insight, and day-to-day community management.

Depending on the shape and structure of the organization, social media activity may fall within the remit of a dedicated social media team or under a broader business unit, such as marketing.

As activity on social channels has become more important for businesses, so too has expertise in how to effectively use the channels. It's unlikely that brands that once would have placed their social media presence in the hands of an inexperienced yet willing intern, would do so now.

In a relatively short period of time, social media management has become a niche area of expertise. Business schools, marketing institutes and training academies now offer specific qualifications just in social media.

Due to the complexities and the range of expertise and experience required, many organizations, chief marketing officers and heads of departments must now consider whether social media is best managed in-house or outsourced to an external specialist agency.

In this myth, we'll explore the strengths and weaknesses of both options, and pose some questions for you to consider with the aim of helping you to gain clarity on this quandary.

In-house team or outsourced solution?

Social media activity isn't purely about 'sticking it on social', scheduling posts and 'filling the feeds'. To optimize activity, strategic thinking, brand messaging and creative campaign alignment is required. Every interaction, post, response, image, video or advertisement on social media is a brand touchpoint. Due to the nature of the channels, these can be:

- sharing brand messaging;
- promoting products or services;
- responding to customer queries, viewpoints or engagement on your posts;

- tracking conversations, brand mentions, reputation and sentiment;
- watching what others in your arena are doing – key partners, competitors, customers and influencers;
- managing targeted social advertising campaigns, engagement and conversation;
- social selling, using the channels for business development and networking;
- recruitment and employer brand messaging.

As you can see from this list (which is by no means exhaustive), when thinking how to best manage your social media presence, there will be different projects, some of which can be managed in-house and some outsourced. It could be that day-to-day brand promotion and community management is managed internally, while paid social advertising campaigns are managed by an external agency.

It helps to be clear on what you want to achieve and, importantly, whether the activity you're looking to embark upon is long-term or short-term. Think about the following:

- How much time do you/your team have to devote to managing social media?
- Do you have the required level of expertise in-house?
- What is it that you are specifically looking for an external agency to achieve (content strategy, creative and development, social media strategy, planning, data, reporting or analytics)? Do you have clarity on the brief?
- Is what you're looking for generalist or specialist? For example, paid advertising on social media or data insights and social media reputation analysis.

- What is the size of your budget? Do you have the scope to increase your headcount or invest in training your current team?
- Is there appetite for the necessary skill development within the team?
- How quickly are you needing to get things started? What's going to fit best with timescales?
- Have you weighed up the pros and cons associated with managing social media activity in-house vs outsourcing it?

Time is one of the biggest reasons businesses look to outsource their social media. Being a socially connected business is a 24/7 effort. In the same way organizations don't turn off their website presence, so too are social channels always on. Keeping your brand in front of customers means consistently dripping content and messages and being responsive. Customers choose to engage at a time that suits them and, as we've discussed in earlier myths, expectations around the speed of response are high.

Your authentic voice

Just as a CEO or leader can't outsource their own voice to build trust (see Myth 22), authenticity of brand voice needs to be considered too.

Whether you are training a team member to manage social media or outsourcing to an external agency or free-lancer, it's critical that a rigorous induction-style process is implemented. In just the same way as when a new team member is welcomed to the business, your external agency needs to know your brand guidelines, what they can and can't say, the tone of voice you use, and any dos and don'ts. It takes time and a bit of mentoring to ensure that the necessary learning is embedded.

Once an agency has been selected, you still need to stay close to what's being said on your social platforms. Learning and trust are things that grow – and blaming your community manager never goes down well.

In 2017 the US Department of Education put out a tweet misspelling the name of civil rights leader, W.E.B. Du Bois (spelling it DeBois) during Black History Month. There was an immediate backlash pointing out the department's sloppiness with many responses stating that they should have had a proper 'teacher' checking the tweets.[1]

Sense-checks and approval

Enterprise social media dashboard tools (as mentioned in Myth 8) enable agencies and in-house teams to share proposed scheduled messages with an approver, so that they can review, edit or make suggestions around language and brand messaging.

Over time, the intention is that those managing the messaging become familiar with tone of voice and what is and isn't permissible, and it may be that the initial approval process becomes more relaxed. This may take the form of the community manager, whether internal or agency-side, sending a quick message on Skype or WhatsApp to check the tone before scheduling.

Of course, if disaster strikes, there's always the 'delete' option – but, again, this requires speedy lines of communication and responsiveness.

Hybrid collaborative solution

You may need to bring in external expertise for specific reasons, for example, to execute a formal social media audit, to help develop a broader social media strategy or to support campaigns where you don't have in-house experience or competence. A hybrid collaborative solution enables you to either train up your team to give them the competence or to work in partnership with an agency on a campaign or project for an agreed period. This model can also be useful in imparting knowledge to internal team members.

Pros and cons

Whether hybrid, in-house or outsourced, the route you choose will be fully dependent on the size and structure of your business, budgets and desired outcome. We've highlighted a few pros and cons.

The pros of staying in-house:

- employees are already clear on brand message, values and dos and don'ts;
- the ability to make changes and respond in real time;
- the opportunity for new content development, picking up latest internal news and developments;
- employees know the customer and already understand how to engage with them.

The cons of in-house management:

- existing staff may not have the time, manpower or expertise;
- employees can develop tunnel vision – failing to think outside the box and bring creative angles to activities;

- employees may be restricted by internal politics;
- you will need to invest in enterprise technologies such as social media management dashboards, analytics or social listening and sentiment analysis tools.

The pros of outsourcing:

- agencies have a broader view of what works and what doesn't work across different campaigns, accounts and industries;
- they have specialist expertise that you can draw upon, and should be up to date with the latest shifts and developments in their industry;
- you can buy in the service flexibly, to fit with budgets and campaign requirements;
- agencies may come up with more creative, 'out of the box' content ideas;
- they will have already invested in the necessary tools and dashboards to facilitate effective management, insight and reporting.

The cons of outsourcing:

- you will need to induct the external agency or freelancer on your brand messaging, values and dos and don'ts;
- effectively, they have to become an extension of your team and so there is an onboarding 'getting to know one another' time period to consider;
- there may be some toing and froing between client and agency to make changes and respond in not-so-real time (to eradicate this, processes need to be put in place so that there is opportunity for immediate contact);

- someone within the business will need to be the partner liaison – working with the agency to share latest news stories, content and updates, and generally steer activity.

Conclusion

Social media can most certainly be managed well in-house, provided that the organization is structured with a dedicated team and has the necessary resource, expertise and time to commit. If this is the case, then the 'authentic voice' of a business is far better coming directly from within the organization.

In contrast, if the organization isn't equipped to manage social media activity and there isn't the appetite or resource to build an in-house team, then working with an agency in either an outsourced or hybrid capacity offers an effective and often cost-effective solution.

Note

1   The Department of Education misspells apology for misspelling W.E.B. Du Bois' name: https://www.huffingtonpost.co.uk/entry/devos-web-dubo is_n_58a09088e4b094a129ebc776 (archived at https://perma.cc/ F6SG-AXDV)

MYTH 12

Social media means my business has to be available 24/7

To manage brand reputation, build relationships with your customers and grow the bottom line through customer service, being responsive and conscious of the time it takes to respond is key.

When it comes to understanding how available your business needs to be on social media, a few factors come into play:

- Analysing which social media channels make sense for you to be active on – (meeting your audiences where they are at).

- Understanding how those channels are used by your audiences, the time they spend on the channels, and typical activity.

- A fundamental understanding of why you want to have a presence on the channels. This is probably the most important thing to consider.

The answer to why you want to have a social media presence should be more than simply 'because everyone else has'. And yes, while it's difficult to find organizations these days that don't have some form of social presence, the decision to participate, and how, should be aligned with the strategic direction of your business. It should be planned for and resourced accordingly.

Remember, no one is forcing your business to be on social media; it's a case of figuring out what works for your business and what's necessary for continued success.

In this myth, we'll explore how people are using social media channels, changing customer expectation levels and the opportunity for setting clear expectations for your audiences. We'll also share insights about the evolving automation technologies, tools and resources that can help you to manage the practicalities of being readily available to your audiences, helping you to consider your position on being always-on, 24/7.

How your audience uses social media

As we've highlighted throughout this book, social media is inseparable from our everyday lives. We've discussed access statistics and typical usage, but to reiterate, 4.62 billion people are actively using social media networks on a day-to-day basis.[1] The latest statistics from Ofcom, the UK's regulatory media body, show that people's online time is growing by around 7 per cent annually. The average UK adult spent 3 hours 37 minutes per day online in 2020 – a rise of 9 minutes since 2019.[2]

Globally, it's reported that the average social media user spends 2 hours 27 minutes each day on social platforms.[3] This equates to approximately one-third of total internet time, and one-seventh of our waking lives.

Time spent on social media varies considerably for different cultures. For example, internet users in Japan spend an average of 48 minutes on social media each day, whereas, at the other extreme, Filipinos average 3 hours 57 minutes. While some specific channels will dominate in different countries, it's likely that the places where all your customers participate, at least some of the time, will include Facebook, Facebook Messenger, YouTube, WhatsApp, Instagram, Twitter, Snapchat, TikTok and LinkedIn.[4]

As to time spent on each channel, a 2022 report from We Are Social identifies the following average usage analysis, based on what people did in 2021:[5]

- Facebook – 19.6 hours/month
- YouTube – 23.7 hours/month
- Facebook Messenger – 3 hours/month
- WhatsApp – 18.6 hours/month
- Instagram – 11.2 hours/month
- Twitter – 5.1 hours/month
- Snapchat – 3 hours/month
- TikTok – 19.6 hours/month

LinkedIn isn't included in this analysis. According to market.us, an average user spends 17 minutes per month on the channel.[6] These statistics give you an indication of average usage, but to get an accurate understanding of your own audience, we recommend you undertake your own analysis. We found there to be a huge number of differing research findings in this area – which are influenced by a range of variables. For example, we know that younger demographics use social media platforms for longer periods of time than older ones.

Various technologies can help you learn more about your audiences, their sentiments and platform preferences. Analytical tools such as Brandwatch, Meltwater and others offer sophisticated deeper insight. You can also explore the basic analytics provided by each of the native social platforms. For example, Facebook's Insights tool can prove informative, and LinkedIn can also provide audience insights, if you have the respective tracking pixels and tags embedded in your website.

What customers want

Social platforms have been inextricably linked with customer service and support since their inception, and while these platforms have evolved considerably since those beginnings, customer service is still a significant part of social media engagement for organizations. In fact, many organizations have consciously manoeuvred their first line of customer service response to be delivered via social media (as discussed in Myth 10).

Let's consider a brand or organization that would ordinarily expect high levels of customer service interaction around complaints, such as wireless carrier solution T-Mobile. Their social platforms show that they make use of both Facebook via a Facebook Messenger chatbot service, and Twitter, with a dedicated @TMobileHelp account to connect and communicate directly with customers.

It's unusual now to find a customer-facing organization that isn't taking advantage of these channels. Supermarkets, transport providers, retail brands, public services, governments, products, service solutions – even if the available social platforms aren't positioned as dedicated support services, empowered customers will instinctively use the channels to raise queries.

A 2018 *Harvard Business Review* article highlights the bottom-line impact of customer responsiveness via social media.[7] Using data from Twitter, the research team set out to test the hypothesis that those customers who have a positive interaction via social media will reward that brand with greater loyalty or will pay a premium price for the product or service.

The research experiment ran across two service industries where there was scope for a significant number of interactions: airlines and wireless carriers. They took a sample of over 400,000 customer-service-related tweets comprising complaints, questions and comments, and monitored progress. Six months after the customers had tweeted the various companies, they were invited to take a brief survey.

The outcomes of the research showed that:

- customers who had interacted with a brand's customer service representative on Twitter were significantly more likely to spend extra with the brand or choose the brand more often;

- customers who received any kind of response were willing to pay more;
- net promoter scores were improved.

It's interesting to note the reaction to receiving any kind of response. This indicates that even a response that wasn't resolving the issue, but simply acknowledging it, was still likely to improve the brand relationship.

Response time is also key

The *Harvard Business Review* study also measured response time. This is an important metric. It found that good service happens fast – and when responses were received within five minutes or less, the customer was willing to pay more.

When it comes to expectation around response times, five minutes may seem unrealistic. However, it depends on the level of response given; remember that any response is better than no response. In the first instance, an automated acknowledgment or question could be offered.

It's reported that 67 per cent of consumers have engaged with a brand via social media for customer service needs – and yet, while we're using social media as a key customer support communication channel, our customer service expectations don't appear to be being met.[8] Further, Hubspot reports that 79 per cent of customers expect brands to respond to their social media posts within 24 hours.[9]

For any organization, it's worth responding – not only to turn around that negative situation as quickly as possible and retain that customer, but also to avoid others being influenced by such posts.

Enter artificial intelligence

While response times required may need to be quicker than those typically delivered via traditional routes, there's also the volume of interactions to consider. Increasingly, artificial intelligence chatbots are being used to engage, filter and create more efficiencies to improve customer service enquiries, far more quickly than could be managed by human customer service agents.

A great example is Facebook's Messenger Chatbot, a friendly and accessible automated messaging software that converses with customers, which can be programmed to understand questions, provide answers and execute tasks such as loading a web page, routing to join a call or sharing a file to download. As well as speedily responding to customers, this automation of information gathering and management of menial tasks frees up time for customer service agents to focus on more involved enquiries.

Another great solution is Cora, the Royal Bank of Scotland's intelligent chatbot.[10] Cora has been programmed to manage over 200 customer intentions and has more than 1,000 responses. It's estimated that Cora answers 5,000 questions a day and understands when 'she' needs to pass the customer across to a human agent – who by then has a documented understanding of the conversation, and is able to assist more speedily.

Setting clear expectations

Of course, while there's an assumption that just having a presence on social media means that you are accessible 24/7, brands and organizations can still manage customer expectation by providing clarity as to when platforms are staffed. For example, the Marks and Spencer Twitter account, @marksandspencer, states very clearly in the header of their bio, the hours that their social media accounts are available:

> Welcome to the official M&S Twitter page. Follow us here for news on our newest food, latest fashion and home inspiration. We're here daily, 8am–10pm.

Such clarity at least gives the customer the understanding that if they send a message at 11 pm, it's unlikely anyone will respond until the morning.

Conclusion

While the myth of needing to be available 24/7 isn't totally busted, the reality is that while social media channels are accessed by billions of people for a growing number of hours per day, your business has full permission to be accessible and engaged in a way that fits with your operating processes.

However, to manage brand reputation, build relationships with your customers and grow the bottom line through customer service, being responsive and conscious of the time it takes to respond is key.

Notes

1   Digital 2021 October global snapshot report: https://datareportal.com/
    reports/digital-2021-october-global-statshot (archived at https://perma.cc/
    X6V8-X8B3)

2   Online Nation: 2021 report: https://www.ofcom.org.uk/__data/assets/
    pdf_file/0013/220414/online-nation-2021-report.pdf (archived at
    https://perma.cc/XSJ4-RQS9)

3   Digital 2022 We Are Social Report: https://wearesocial.com/uk/
    blog/2022/01/digital-2022/ (archived at https://perma.cc/8WHN-ATLS)

4   How long do people spend on social media? https://techjury.net/blog/
    time-spent-on-social-media/ (archived at https://perma.cc/38M4-
    DGYX)

5   Digital 2022 We Are Social Report: https://wearesocial.com/uk/
    blog/2022/01/digital-2022/ (archived at https://perma.cc/8WHN-ATLS)

6   LinkedIn statistics and facts: https://market.us/statistics/social-media/
    linkedin/ (archived at https://perma.cc/UH7A-6FSZ)

7   How customer service can turn angry customers into loyal ones: https://
    hbr.org/2018/01/how-customer-service-can-turn-angry-customers-into-
    loyal-ones (archived at https://perma.cc/ADN8-2U5E)

8   6 key elements of using social media for customer service: https://
    freshsparks.com/using-social-media-for-customer-service (archived at
    https://perma.cc/F9DS-DUNJ)

9   What are your customers' expectations for social media response time?
    https://blog.hubspot.com/service/social-media-response-time (archived
    at https://perma.cc/TLA4-PR88)

10 Birth of a digital assistant – teaching Cora: https://mediacenter.ibm.com/
    media/1_ujpeoiga?mhsrc=ibmsearch_a&mhq=teaching%20cora
    (archived at https://perma.cc/B6GC-EZTZ)

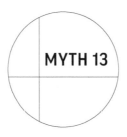

MYTH 13

Social media is no use for internal communications

As the boundaries between the social platforms we use in our personal lives and the tools and resources we use in our working lives continue to blend, it makes sense for social networking technologies to be optimized across organizations.

As social technologies have evolved, and adoption and usage of the platforms has increased, the use of social media within organizations to aid their own internal communications has become more commonplace.

There is an increasing body of evidence which shows that social technologies are fast developing as an internal resource, helping organizations to become more collaborative, creative and connected. The growth of these internal social networks is driving a sense of belonging and community among employees, and assisting with very tangible improvements in employee engagement, productivity, innovation and ultimately profitability.

In this myth we'll explore the rise of internal social media usage for business, and how social media technologies used internally are helping organizations to break down organizational and operational silos, drive innovation, save time and enable employees and teams to collaborate more effectively.

The potential benefits

Improving the productivity and effectiveness of people within organizations has been a hot topic since business began.

At a time when we have more communication channels at our fingertips than ever before, the challenge of low productivity and employee disengagement continues to rise. According to Gallup, only 20 per cent of the workforce is engaged at work. Just 11 per cent of Western European workers are generally engaged, compared with 34 per cent of those in the US and Canada. Give the turmoil caused by the Covid-19 pandemic, it is perhaps unsurprising that employee engagement decreased by two percentage points between 2019 and 2020, following a steady rise over the last decade.[1]

While the 2021 Gallup report is largely focused on the toll the pandemic took on the workforce, a previous report has highlighted that lack of engagement and low productivity can be largely attributed to unnecessary admin and poor communication:

- the average worker spends 13 hours a week on emails alone, which means 28 per cent of the working week is taken up by email management;
- 86 per cent of corporate executives, employees and educators say that ineffective communication is a big reason for failures in the workplace;
- 58 per cent say poor management is the biggest challenge getting in the way of productivity.[2]

It's inspiring to learn, then, that many organizations are turning to internal social media technologies to connect employees in a far more effective way. One example is France-based information technology services firm Atos Origin. The company, which has more than 70,000 employees across 40 territories, introduced an internal social network to the workplace, reducing the use of email by 60 per cent across the organization. The objective is to turn Atos into a zero-email company.[3]

The introduction of social technologies is reported to have improved the sharing of knowledge across the enterprise, making it easier to locate subject matter experts and, importantly, allow for more efficient collaboration. McKinsey Global Institute reports a rise in productivity of workers of 20–25 per cent when using social media technologies to enhance communications, knowledge sharing and collaboration.[4]

As well as productivity, there's also the opportunity to unlock talent and knowledge within organizations to drive innovation. A research article by ACAS described an example from South Eastern Railway, who turned to social technologies to connect and communicate with their dispersed employee base of around 4,000 people.[5] They developed a bespoke social network, which brought their staff together to deal with work issues, and provided a sense of 'voice' to employees so they could more easily speak out, alert others to challenges, get answers and provide solutions to others.

Another aspect of the Covid-19 pandemic, as reported by McKinsey, was the acceleration of digital transformation, with more organizations having to utilize online networks to connect and collaborate their 'home bound' teams.[6] According to research from Deloitte, the mass adoption of digital technology has created two digital workplaces operating in parallel with the physical. The *personal* digital workplace blends an employee's own devices and services with those provided by the organization. *Shared* digital workplaces are those enabled by interconnected, networked digital technologies where employees interact with their teammates.[7] These include enterprise social technologies such as Slack, Chatter, Yammer and Meta (previously Facebook, Inc) Workplace. Meta highlight several case studies across a range of businesses, such as Virgin Atlantic, showing the importance of the platform as a critical communications tool during the pandemic. AstraZeneca uses Workplace for internal collaboration, connecting 64,000 of their people to harness the power of community at work, including the entire leadership team.[8]

As logical as it seems to connect employees via internal social networks to enable them to work more collaboratively, the use of internal social media is currently far from mainstream.

The challenges of internal social media

The lack of mainstream adoption may be aligned with challenges companies face when implementing new technologies. The usual education and behavioural changes required to adopt a new way of doing things can cause friction. A solution is to take a social approach at the outset – involve employees, canvass their opinions and co-create a solution.

The role of leadership

Another potential challenge relates to leadership, and the related cultural and operational shifts required to develop a more connected and collaborative workforce. Such organizational and people management elements run far deeper than simply deciding which internal social media technology to select and ensuring teams are trained effectively. These shifts need to be driven from the top of the organization – which brings us to exploring the role leadership plays – an area we explore further in Myth 22.

Roland Deiser, Director at the Center for the Future of Organization at the Drucker School of Management, in a podcast interview with the authors, referred to social technologies as 'hierarchy busters'.[9] To reap the benefits of internal social technologies, organizations need to develop or transform internal structures and operations to become more open, flatter and non-hierarchical and to create a culture of trust.

A study by Ashridge Leadership Education and Hult International Business School highlights the advantage social media offers as a tool for organizations to improve agility, interaction, content-sharing, knowledge and collaboration.[10] It also focuses on how social channels improve leadership effectiveness by enforcing clarity and transparency of communication – increasing speed, breadth and, importantly, intimacy to enhance the relationship between leaders and followers.

The Ashridge study further identifies that internal social media communication makes clarity around organizational strategy highly necessary. This point was elaborated upon in another podcast interview by the authors with the lead researcher of the Ashridge Study, Professor Patricia Hinds. She discussed how the use of social media within organizations was shining a light on the necessary clarity of organizational strategy – driving leaders and those tasked with communicating strategy and purpose throughout organizations to create consistent and clear lines of communication.[11]

Paul Frampton Calero, ex-CEO of Havas Group, also shared some examples with us demonstrating how social technology was critical in keeping him connected with his employee base around the world. It not only enabled him to connect and regularly tune in to employee voice, regardless of geography, but also gave voice to those employees that he either wouldn't ordinarily get to meet or who wouldn't feel confident to speak out in a room.

Implementation – the practicalities

The blistering rate of technological advancement and digital transformation continues to impact society and organizations. We've talked about the adoption rates of mainstream social networks, and so too how the tools we choose to connect and communicate externally also permeate our working environments.

After all, in just the same way as they give individuals opportunity to tune in and reach out to anyone and share their voice outside an organization, so too do internal social networks provide the same opportunity – not only for employees, but for leaders and CEOs too.

This together with the associated growth in the importance of agility and collaboration to organizational success, means it's likely that internal social networks will indeed become even more mainstream and business-as-usual as we continue to navigate the future of work.

There are some associated practicalities to consider:

- Lead from the top, as touched on in Myth 22. Get senior leaders on board, allowing others within the organization to engage and embrace a more social way of communicating.
- Have a clear objective as to the challenge your internal social network is looking to solve/improve – and work from that starting point. If there isn't compelling reason for people to use the channels, they won't.
- Research which channels your teams are familiar with and what's going to work with your organizational culture. For example, if 99 per cent of your workforce use

Facebook socially, then Workplace may be the perfect fit. The key is to get your teams involved from a user research perspective, to co-create effective solutions.

Engaging employees

In a Queens University of Charlotte survey, 80 per cent of Millennials (aged 18–29) would prefer real-time feedback over traditional performance reviews, 89 per cent of them use social networks as communication tools in the workplace, and 40 per cent would even pay for social tools to use within the workplace to increase efficiency.[12]

Top-performing organizations are building community – fostering the sense that employees at all levels are in it together. These organizations are creating the opportunity for social interactions using the latest new media technologies. Those that do this well typically see improved productivity levels and better financial performance.

For the employer, engagement is about positive attitudes, drawing on employees' knowledge and skills for improvement, better communication, and making sure the company's values are consistent and respected.

Conclusion

The myth that social media is no good for internal communications has been well and truly disproved. As the boundaries between the social platforms we use in our personal lives and the tools and resources we use in our working lives continue to blend, it makes sense for social networking technologies to be optimized across organizations.

Notes

1 State of the global workplace 2021 report: https://www.gallup.com/workplace/349484/state-of-the-global-workplace.aspx (archived at https://perma.cc/58GQ-FSKE)

2 Just one in 10 Brits feel engaged at work, says Gallup: www.peoplemanagement.co.uk/news/articles/one-in-10-brits-engaged-work (archived at https://perma.cc/8BZP-YYPW)

3 Why Atos origin is striving to be a zero-email company: www.forbes.com/sites/davidburkus/2016/07/12/why-atos-origin-is-striving-to-be-a-zero-email-company (archived at https://perma.cc/679N-HM23)

4 The social economy: Unlocking value and productivity through social technologies: www.mckinsey.com/industries/technology-media-and-telecommunications/our-insights/the-social-economy (archived at https://perma.cc/2UB8-M6DL)

5 Employee engagement: Decoding social media for the workplace: www.hrzone.com/perform/business/employee-engagement-decoding-social-media-for-the-workplace (archived at https://perma.cc/67SN-Y2BD)

6 How Covid-19 has pushed companies over the technology tipping point – and transformed business forever: https://www.mckinsey.com/business-functions/strategy-and-corporate-finance/our-insights/how-covid-19-has-pushed-companies-over-the-technology-tipping-point-and-transformed-business-forever (archived at https://perma.cc/8PUK-EBQ9)

7 The digital-ready workplace: https://www2.deloitte.com/global/en/insights/focus/technology-and-the-future-of-work/supercharging-teams-in-the-digital-workplace.html (archived at https://perma.cc/8DQL-EP25)

8 Workplace case studies: www.facebook.com/workplace/case-studies (archived at https://perma.cc/M8SR-A2RT)

9   The connected leader podcast: www.carvillcreative.co.uk/podcasts
     (archived at https://perma.cc/KE3M-6H43)
10   Leadership in an age of social media: www.hrmagazine.co.uk/
     article-details/leadership-in-an-age-of-social-media (archived at https://
     perma.cc/C9QT-T9BH)
11   Get social – the connected leader podcast: https://open.spotify.com/epi
     sode/2miDbWTYCKnkAV7hJHKoqT?si=5Pm2yGq_QMKr_
     dhvzIsjHw&nd=1 (archived at https://perma.cc/6UGW-HPK4)
12   Communicating in the modern workplace: https://online.queens.edu/
     resources/infographic/communicating-in-the-workplace/ (archived at
     https://perma.cc/ZGJ4-PX4X)

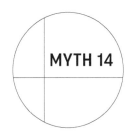

MYTH 14

Employees know what is expected of them on social media

There is an enormous difference between using social media personally and on behalf of your organization. Guidelines need to clearly stipulate what is deemed 'acceptable use' when at work or using the company name in association with personal profiles.

Social media offers seemingly limitless opportunities to connect and collaborate with other people, to find new audiences and to expand traditional ones. There are billions of users and hundreds of billions of social media accounts. As we saw in Myth 2, social media users have an average of 7.5 accounts.[1] Many companies run dozens or even hundreds of social media accounts.

Getting noticed on social media is about standing out, differentiating yourself, and finding ways of attracting attention. A report by LinkedIn emphasizes the importance of this for employers: differentiating your company from the competition is essential for companies that want to attract the best employees – with more than half of companies saying that the biggest challenge they face in recruiting is competition for talent.[2]

The same advice is given for job seekers: distinguish yourself from the competition and create a 'personal brand'. This becomes increasingly challenging when there are billions of people trying to do the same thing. A viral post, a great piece of content or a channel with popular appeal can turn success in digital communications into success in other domains.

And yet, getting attention online is not always a useful, positive, or desirable experience. People and companies often get noticed for the wrong reasons. Strong negative emotions tend to the be the most powerful viral catalyst on social media. Some people will choose to use this in a deliberate and calculating way online. Many others find their content is received in ways that were not originally intended, their message is misused or misinterpreted, and in extreme circumstances, people can find themselves targets of social media mobs (see Myth 20). While social media can be an incredibly useful tool, there is a sharp and dangerous side to it and it's not always possible to predict how your audience or the wider social media sphere will react to your activity.

As an employer and employee, it is important to be aware of this darker side of getting noticed on social media and the negative impact that online social activity can have. There is an enormous difference between using social media personally and on behalf of your organization. Guidelines need to clearly stipulate what is deemed 'acceptable use' when at work or using the company name in association with personal profiles.

The risk of the blue tick demographic

One of the advantages of social networks is that many users post their thoughts publicly online. This creates an enormous amount of data which companies can use to analyse general trends in consumer behaviour and public opinion. Analysis can give insight into how users feel about a certain brand, person or idea at a single point in time or over time. It's an expansion of the old political focus group, where, for example, a pre-selected demographic might have been asked to rate their feelings about a political speech. This is particularly true of Twitter where a great deal of political and social discussion happens, with participation from journalists, politicians and social commentators.

While this all sounds great, there are limitations to using this insight, which employees need to be made aware of. The culture on your favourite social media platform may be radically different from the culture in a workplace. The same problem persists that researchers have encountered for years: is this sample group representative of the wider population as a whole, or the group of people they are interested in? If you pull a group of people out of a fast-food restaurant, a supermarket, a social club or a pub, you cannot be sure that they are representative of the entire population. It may be that there are certain traits, characteristics, interests or other factors that bring people together, and these are often factors that influence opinion. The same is true of social media sites such as Twitter, which tends to be full of extreme and controversial views, but is not always a good representation of the attitudes of the general population.

Research indicates that social media users are not representative of the general population. In the United States, for example, Twitter users tend to be younger, have more post-secondary educational qualifications, have higher incomes and are more liberal than the general population.[3] And even among these users, there are differences. Most people barely say anything online, while 10 per cent of users generate 80 per cent of all tweets. These prolific tweeters are different from the overall Twitter user base, and even further from the population average, being much more likely to be women, and to post about political subjects.

In just the same way that social media users aren't representative of the general population, neither are users on one platform representative of users on another. In Myths 2 and 26 we discuss how different social platforms have different purposes, different audiences and different social expectations. Culture varies between groups and platforms and each has their own quirks. While these platforms can be extraordinarily useful for reaching their user base, do not assume that any social media platform is automatically a good gauge of general trends, or of the opinions of all people.

Recommendations for workplace social media policy

Every employee is likely to have their own preferred social media platforms which combine to form a collection of their own groups and communities. They are also likely to have differing interpretations of how much work and social media should intersect. For this reason, it's essential to have a shared understanding and some formalized policy or guidelines about workplace social media use. This policy should describe what kind of online behaviours could cause problems for the company externally (for example, photos taken while in a company uniform, personal posts to a company's page or personal posts about professional relationships). What follows are six recommendations for a workplace social media policy:

1 **Have a clear policy for resolving disputes outside social media.**
   Disagreements are bound to happen in the workplace, and there should be a clear and accessible way to manage these disputes in a constructive way. Complaining about colleagues, gossiping, and posting grievances on social media is much more likely to occur when employees do not have a more fair and constructive way to manage disputes and resolve problems. Effective HR and management practices to help manage this are crucial.

2 **Clearly define what information is confidential.**
   Certain workplace information should never be posted publicly or even privately to someone's social media page or an external site. Typically, this includes confidential

information such as client information, business plans, personnel data and intellectual property.

Remember that some information that seems innocuous may also be confidential – for example, accidentally revealing location history, meeting dates, diary appointments or tagging other people in a post has the potential to give away sensitive information (see Myth 28). Clearly define what information is considered confidential to avoid employees making innocent mistakes.

3 **Designate a specific person to answer questions.**

Many people find it difficult to keep track of all the information they are sharing online and some people will find social media etiquette and company policies confusing. Designate a specific person who is both knowledgeable and approachable to give friendly advice about company policy and social media. Employees will appreciate being able to access this advice. It also disqualifies the old 'No one told me that was a bad idea before I did it' argument.

4 **Provide positive examples of how to engage with others online.**

This is particularly important, because providing models of desirable and effective behaviour in the workplace tends to be more effective than long lists and policy manuals of no-nos. Give examples of how people have managed conflict, used social media to get information effectively, or used the technology in an admirable way. Remember that even people who have a great deal of experience with personal social media may have never used it for professional purposes before.

5 **Clearly explain what is illegal and unethical online.**
There are some obvious examples here – no hate speech, no bigoted language, and don't threaten or harass people online. But there may be more nuanced issues, such as how and where employees can use the company logo or copyrighted materials online. Can employees use a picture of themselves in a company uniform or at a company-branded site on their social media page? If so, are there added expectations for their conduct online?

6 **Clarify the consequences of certain actions.**
This is no different to any other workplace policy. Stealing, bullying or harassment in the workplace should all carry consequences, and this should apply equally if bad behaviour occurs on social media.
Minor mistakes or slip-ups may only require a quick chat, and an explanation of how to handle the situation better next time. More destructive or antisocial behaviour should have clear consequences.

Conclusion

Don't assume that employees know what is expected of them on social media. There are distinct differences between personal and professional use and every work-place which uses social media should have a clear policy in place to protect both the company and the people who work there.

Notes

1   Digital 2022 We Are Social Report: https://wearesocial.com/uk/
    blog/2022/01/digital-2022/ (archived at https://perma.cc/K34C-6DBR)
2   Global recruiting trends 2017: What you need to know about the state
    of talent acquisition: https://business.linkedin.com/talent-solutions/cx/
    2016/10/ global-recruiting-trends-2017 (archived at https://perma.cc/
    2NY7-LS8Q)
3   Sizing up Twitter users: www.pewinternet.org/2019/04/24/sizing-up-
    twitter-users (archived at https://perma.cc/2FXX-Z4CC)

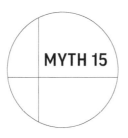

MYTH 15

Social media is not effective for business development

Social media can play a significant part in keeping sales and business development professionals fully informed of the latest news and developments of any prospective organizations or key persons within those organizations.

In previous myths we've talked about the role of social media across a business. This myth dives a little deeper into one area where many organizations, particularly those in the B2B landscape, are keen to optimize social media – business development.

It's easy to see how the visibility of connections online can expand opportunity for building new connections via social networks for business. This is commonly referred to as 'social selling'. It is the act of leveraging your social network connections to find new and relevant prospects, with an intention of building trusted relationships. The aim is to leverage those relationships to achieve business objectives and sales targets. Effectively, it's simply good old-fashioned business networking and building trust – but doing so purely online. The social networks enable businesses to keep in touch with clients, partners and potential clients regularly. This eradicates the awkward cold call and isn't restricted by geographical location.

LinkedIn's 2021 State of Sales report identified that during the Covid-19 pandemic, virtual selling became the main means of selling. Given restrictions, it was the only way to reach prospects – and their survey found that 74 per cent of sellers said they were committed to expanding their LinkedIn network as it had become a primary source of demand generation.

The same research further identified sales behaviours that were damaging sales conversion, namely:

- 48 per cent of buyers felt they were given misleading information about a product, for example its price;
- 44 per cent of buyers felt the seller didn't understand their company and its needs;
- 43 per cent of buyers felt the seller didn't understand their own product or service.[1]

Clearly, these damaging behaviours can be improved upon considerably when sales and business development professionals use social media. Content and information that is regularly shared from the corporate LinkedIn profile can be automatically disseminated to business development and sales professionals on the team. They can share it to their own feeds, along with their own subject matter expertise, thus eradicating any misleading information. Of course, this also helps team members better understand the nuances of their own product or service, continuously staying up to speed and in tune with latest developments.

The benefits of social selling

As outlined above, sales success can be hampered if the seller doesn't fully understand the prospect's company and its needs. Social media can play a significant part in keeping sales and business development professionals fully informed of the latest news and developments of any prospective organizations or key persons within those organizations. Once networked and connected, or once following an organization or person, the platforms enable the user to not only share content and insights, but importantly to tune in and listen to the latest updates and developments. The opportunity to see first-hand updates and news from prospective organizations helps sales professionals to stay relevant and connected to the needs of the organizations they are looking to serve. Indeed, the LinkedIn State of Sales report highlights:

> Top-performing salespeople spend far more of their time researching their industry, learning about their competitors, understanding trends, reading about ancillary things that affect their industry and being thought leaders and consultants in their space than they do pounding phones, sending emails, and prospecting (Sahil Mansuri, CEO, Bravado).

New social links can start out loosely over weeks, months and sometimes years of networking, collaborating, sharing and conversing online. Over time, those loose links strengthen to become more meaningful networks which are often clustered around the founding topic or interest.

As authors, we converse on the topic of social media on Twitter using the hashtag #socialceo, which has resulted in moving relationships from online to offline interviews, meetings and collaboration. This is a simple example of loose connections talking about the same topic coming together to strengthen connections into something far more significant than a collection of tweets.

There's also evidence that taking the time to engage with social selling reaps rewards. Salesforce reports that 78 per cent of social sellers outsell peers who don't use social media, and 39 per cent of business-to-business professionals said that they were able to reduce account and contact research time using social media.[2]

The practicalities of social selling

There are many articles and books that dive far deeper into 'social selling' than we have the space to in this myth (one book we recommend is *Social Selling* by Tim Hughes[3]). Here we'll give a brief overview of the practicalities that need to be thought through to successfully use social media for relationship building and business development. While the techniques needed to optimize connection and engagement may differ from platform to platform, the key drivers are the same. Social media platforms enable you to:

- Listen in to the changing needs of your prospective customers/partners. You can look out for changes in structure, expansion projects, new developments, new team members and track these changes organically via your social media feeds. It's a good idea to set a regular time in your diary to reacquaint yourself with any potential opportunities, and you may want to do this daily. This may be to simply congratulate someone on a new award or milestone. Just as we drop our friends a line to see how they're doing and show we care, the same familiarity, with context, can continuously build those human connections. If you have several prospective customers to stay acquainted with, it can be useful to set 'alerts' on social listening platforms, or use social media dashboards to centralize news and updates from prospects. Even simple Google Alerts can be a useful tool in helping you to stay on top of key topics.

- Listen in to any gripes, complaints or challenges your prospective customer may be talking about, or any specific pain points or grumbles that you know your product or service can support. Just a friendly, 'been there, understand your challenge, this is how we overcame it' conversation can help to cement the view that you're listening and are concerned and keen to help where you can. Research shows that 62 per cent of customers say they share bad customer experiences with others online.[4] Listening in can help you to spot those grumbles and either rectify or empathize. The same research shows that 72 per cent of customers say they share good experiences online. This gives you the opportunity to either celebrate with them, or gain some intel into what has gone so well for them.

· Listen in to competitor activity which helps you to stay on top of the landscape you're operating in.

· Share content that meets the needs of your audiences in a timely, relevant and (ideally) human way. If you hear them mention something, use it as an opportunity to share a useful article or your subject matter expertise by way of a post or a private message.

Of course, the key to using social media platforms for listening in and sharing content and advice is to keep it relevant and human. You don't want to simply 'push' messaging all the time to audiences in a spammy sales way, but rather focus on and meet their needs. Share information you know they're going to be interested in, with the aim of bringing all these moving parts together to build trusted relationships.

Conclusion

When used the right way, social media can be highly effective for business development. In the world of hyperconnected communications facilitated by social media, the famous sales line from the 1980s film, *Glengarry Glen Ross*, 'Always be closing' should be repositioned. Shift focus from 'Always be closing' to 'Always be helping'.[5]

Notes

1 LinkedIn State of Sales Report 2021: https://www.linkedin.com/
business/sales/blog/trends/the-linkedin-state-of-sales-report-2021
(archived at https://perma.cc/D4UV-P7Z8)

2 What is social selling and how does it work?: https://www.salesforce.
com/blog/guide-to-social-selling/ (archived at https://perma.cc/ZR69-
ZP8Z)

3 Hughes, T and Reynolds, M (2016) *Social Selling: Techniques to
influence buyers and changemakers*, Kogan Page, London

4 What is social selling and how does it work?: https://www.salesforce.
com/blog/guide-to-social-selling/ (archived at https://perma.cc/9PEF-
8E5E)

5 It's time to move from 'Always Be Closing' to this new sales mantra,
Hubspot: https://blog.hubspot.com/sales/always-be-closing-is-dead-how-
to-always-be-helping-in-2015 (archived at https://perma.cc/56EB-F5L4)

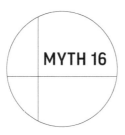

MYTH 16

It's not possible to measure social media ROI

Each activity on a social channel should have set objectives and a clear purpose. Only once you have identified metrics that really matter can you have any idea whether you are hitting targets.

Social media return on investment (ROI) continues to be a keenly debated topic. A 2021 study undertaken by Sprout Social found that only 15 per cent of marketers use social data to measure ROI.[1]

So, what's the magic formula for ROI? What should people be measuring when it comes to social media and what returns should they expect to see?

Today, in all realms of digital marketing we've got data coming out of our data, and in recent years there has been an explosion of technologies that enable businesses to track and monitor every move a customer makes. In this myth, we'll talk about what organizations need to consider to effectively measure ROI.

Big data well and truly exists

According to Statista, data creation will be over 180 zetta-bytes by 2025 – an increase of approximately 118.8 zettabytes from 2020. The numbers are mind-blowing, particularly when you consider what a zettabyte looks like (1,000,000,000,000,000,000,000 bytes!).[2]

The tools that provide us with the ability to continu-ously monitor and measure activity across digital and social media have enabled an equally mind-blowing array of metrics, often to a very granular level. For example, it's one thing to understand 'brand sentiment', and whether the conversation is positive or negative. It's another to drill into the context of that sentiment, considering aspects such as 'brand passion' – measuring levels and consistency of positive feelings.

However, just because we can measure something, doesn't necessarily mean we receive useful or meaningful results. This is particularly true when it comes to measur-ing ROI.

Measuring ROI is relatively simple for businesses that can align their social media metrics directly to financial gains. For example, when a direct-to-consumer brand invests £10,000 exclusively in Facebook advertising and tracks £30,000 in related online sales, they know the monetary return on their social media efforts.

To gain a true measure of the fundamental return on your investment, it's crucial to have clarity from the get-go on what you want to achieve. This will help you determine metrics that matter. We like the not-so-famous quote by US sales trainer and motivational legend, Zig Ziglar: 'Those that aim for nothing hit it with remarkable accuracy.'

With each of the popular social channels, whether Facebook, Instagram, Twitter, Pinterest, LinkedIn, YouTube, TikTok or Snapchat – it's fair to conclude that they collect, store and publish a lot of data. Much of it is highly visible and, therefore, pretty simple to measure. Data such as the number of followers, reposts, shares, comments, likes – and other such forms of engagement – provide us with some very basic measurement opportunities.

This top-line data, often referred to as 'social signals', offers more of a temperature check as to how content, campaigns and messages are landing with audiences, rather than providing metrics related to overarching objectives aligned with organizational strategy.

For example, if the objective of a campaign is to grow the baseline of the number of followers a business, brand or account has, then it's very simple to see whether activity moves the dial. While simple, there will be times where such basic metrics are both useful and meaningful; for example, at the outset of a campaign, it may be useful to measure whether the number of people following and engaging is expanding or decreasing.

The sheer potential volume of activity, speed and real-time visibility enables teams to pivot and switch tactics if metric markers show that activity is having a negative impact. For example, a leading tech manufacturing organization noticed that during one social advertising campaign, the number of followers across their social media accounts started to quickly decline. It was very apparent that something within the campaign wasn't landing. While the basic metric didn't tell them specifically why the decline was happening, it did provide the necessary insights to review the campaign and address any issues, such as the volume of ads shown, the actual message within the campaign, and the ad timings.

What you measure is contextual

This very basic example shines a light on the larger challenge when it comes to measuring social media activity and social media ROI.

Social technologies are used throughout organizations in different ways. Depending on the focus of the organization, and as discussed further in Myth 10, social media activity could affect a range of departments: customer service, HR/recruitment teams, PR and marketing, business development and sales, and R&D.

Therefore, what you measure and at what point, becomes highly dependent on the context in which social media activity is being carried out, and how it relates to relevant and specific departmental objectives.

For example, for customer service teams, metrics for social media success may focus on speed of response, reduction of escalated incidents or positive sentiment. For marketing, they may look at brand awareness, share of voice, influencer outreach, lead generation or reputation management.

Social media may be supporting and influencing many factors, from brand awareness, new audience engagement, reach of audience, share of voice, website visits, content dissemination and influencer engagement through to more specific value creation such as lead generation, email capture and downloads, as well as direct sales.

Social media is now a major influence on consumer purchasing habits. Insider Intelligence's Social Commerce Report estimates that about half of all US adults made a purchase via social media in 2021. And according to a GlobalWebIndex survey, 70 per cent of US internet users who regularly watch influencer-led livestreams are likely to buy the recommended products.[3] However, measuring direct sales is far easier than measuring influence.

From an ROI perspective, the traditional calculation – resource allocated (time, money, people) deducted from the value created – isn't as clear-cut when it comes to social media activity. The challenge with social media activity is that 'value created' may refer to many things, including intangible and difficult-to-align-with-directly hard metrics such as revenue generated.

Social media thought leader, Gary Vaynerchuk, illustrates the challenge of measuring social media ROI with the interesting question, 'What's the ROI of your mother?' Clearly, it's open to subjectivity.

Aligning social objectives with organizational goals

According to a Sprout Social study, only 36 per cent of marketers cite business goals and objectives as a factor influencing their approach to social. Not only that, but marketers cite measuring ROI and aligning social strategy with other parts of the business among their 10 greatest challenges. To measure value, you need to set social media objectives that are aligned with business and departmental goals.[4]

As highlighted earlier, these objectives may be highly contextual to each campaign or activity, and may change as they progress. To provide a basic steer, Table 16.1 gives a very simple framework aligning organizational or departmental objectives with specific targets (key performance indicators or KPIs) – providing a baseline to measure success against.

TABLE 16.1 Organizational objectives with example social KPIs

Organizational/ departmental objective	Example social media metric (KPI)
Generate new sales lead opportunities	Deliver 20 trial sign-ups per month
Reduce customer service complaint escalation incidents	Reduce average response time on social to under 45 minutes by end of quarter
Increase awareness of new product prior to launch	Boost mentions and conversational buzz around product launch, creating +10% share of voice by end of quarter

It's clear from the basic example framework that to link social media activity to business outcomes, it's important to set specific related targets. This ensures clarity on both what you're measuring and how it relates to business objectives. Pose the right questions at the outset:

- What does success look like?
- What objectives/outcomes are we looking to achieve?
- What metrics/evidence do we need so that we can measure progress?
- What discipline will we apply to ensure we are continuously monitoring and learning?

Once you know what it is that you want to achieve and what those metrics/KPIs look like, you can start to apply a monetary value to them to work out exactly how social media ROI translates commercially.

Dark social – measuring intangible ROI

While we do need to scope specific objectives and the related KPIs for social media activity to measure ROI, there is also a healthy dose of intangible value created by social media activity.

The same challenges experienced when measuring mediums such as PR or advertising campaigns also play out with social media. Just as we can't directly measure the revenue-generating impact of eyeballs on a billboard, so too is it impossible to accurately measure the impact of social media attribution.

We can track granular actions via sophisticated analytics, as well as viewing shares, mentions, comments and other visible forms of engagement. We can't accurately define metrics around, for example, those that read reviews or receive business referrals or product recommendations from friends via a social network, but then visit our website later via another medium, such as a Google search, to take action. Referred to as 'dark social' – traffic that can't be tracked – this creates a challenge when measuring social media ROI.

The other intangible that is difficult to measure is the value of building relationships with audiences on social media. There are many statistics that show the relationship between social media engagement with a brand and purchase loyalty. For example, a 2021 Harris Poll conducted on behalf of Sprout Social found that:

- 55 per cent of consumers rely on social media to learn about brands or companies;
- 35 per cent name social media as the primary way they learn about new products, services or brands;
- 78 per cent will buy from a brand and 77 per cent will chose a brand over a competitor after a positive experience with that brand on social media.[5]

In line with social commerce gaining more traction, e-commerce organizations measure visitors that come to their sites via social media. MADE.com, the furniture retailer, identified that visitors to its site from organic social had an average order value 4 per cent higher than the site's average.[6]

Social media has been a movable feast since its inception. The content, strategies and channels which prove effective today may not prove as effective tomorrow, and the same applies for the metrics you choose to measure ROI against.

It's necessary to stay close to how social media is performing so that teams and organizations can continuously learn and iterate. It's important to remain contextual and agile, yet at the same time realistic in how valuable and viable the metrics you're tracking are. To that end, it's worth sense-checking the following when deciding on metrics:

- Is the metric useful? Does it steer/support decision making?
- Do you have the capacity to measure it effectively?
- Is there a clear reason why you are measuring it?
- Does it align with/feed into your overall business objectives?

Clarify your objectives by asking:

- What does success look like? What objectives/outcomes are we looking to achieve?
- What evidence do we need to measure progress?
- What discipline will we apply to ensure we are continuously monitoring and learning?

Conclusion

Measuring social media ROI is indeed possible – each activity on a social channel should have set objectives and a clear purpose. Only once you have identified metrics that really matter – and have set off with the end in mind – can you have any idea whether you are hitting targets. (Remember that quote from Zig Ziglar!).

Notes

1   How to define an actionable social media ROI for your business: https://
    sproutsocial.com/insights/social-media-roi/ (archived at https://perma.cc/
    S6VN-4P2Q)

2   25+ impressive big data statistics for 2022: https://techjury.net/blog/
    big-data-statistics/#gref (archived at https://perma.cc/WT4B-8UMB)

3   Social commerce 2022: https://www.insiderintelligence.com/insights/
    social-commerce-brand-trends-marketing-strategies/ (archived at
    https://perma.cc/N6NW-BYX5)

4   The Sprout Social Index, Edition XVI: Above & beyond: https://media.
    sproutsocial.com/uploads/2020-Sprout-Social-Index-Above-and-Beyond.pdf
    (archived at https://perma.cc/B4EP-RB62)

5   The future of social media: New data for 2021 and beyond: https://
    sproutsocial.com/insights/data/harris-insights-report/ (archived at
    https://perma.cc/GLA7-3CYT)

6   MADE.COM on the value of social commerce: https://econsultancy.com/
    made-com-on-the-value-of-social-commerce (archived at https://perma.cc/
    RV63-5GTH)

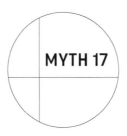

Digital natives are all social media experts

Although there may be some crossover in knowledge and experience, don't assume experience in using social media for personal communication will translate into expertise in its professional use.

There can be a general assumption that groups of people of a similar age share certain traits, values and skills. These gross generalizations are not accurate when it comes to age groups: there is far more psychological variation within any generation than there are clear-cut differences between certain age ranges. One common belief is that because younger people grew up with computers, smartphones, easy access to the internet and social media, they are naturally proficient at using all technology in any capacity. It is true that younger people grow up more familiar with the technology and devices that are popular at the time. But it certainly doesn't mean that all young people are proficient users of every device that has a computer chip, nor does it mean that skills people develop for personal use necessarily translate well into the workplace.

It's necessary to remember that someone's age alone is not a very good predictor of their proficiency in any skill. Some of the most proficient users of any technology will be the creators and inventors. It's more helpful to think of technology as an extension of other real-world domains. Is someone a highly proficient networker and communicator? If so, it's likely that proficiency will extend to social media.

There is also some concern that young people's tech proficiency is now declining. Most hardware and software design is now supposed to be 'frictionless' so no longer requires any technical expertise to operate. There is a new cohort of commentators who bemoan the lack of tech literacy... 'young people now have terrible tech skills'.

The problem with age stereotypes

Most stereotypes based on age or generational differences are false. Aging has a few biological realities that are impossible to deny, but in terms of personality, attitudes, beliefs, values, skills, knowledge and proficiency, generational stereotypes have little merit. There certainly are many young people who are proficient social media users, and of course there are older people who have little to no understanding of social media. But assuming that age is an accurate predictor of social media proficiency in the workplace is a mistake.

Most of the stereotypes about younger (and older) workers do not stand up to scrutiny. The book *Myths of Work* takes a systemic approach to debunking common myths about younger (and older) generations. Younger workers are sometimes assumed to be lazy, social media-obsessed narcissists, while older workers are painted as dogmatic, resistant to change and slow to learn. The research from hundreds of scientific studies looking at hundreds of thousands of workers finds no evidence that either stereotype is true. The book concludes: 'There are no significant generational differences [...] in the workplace and there are far better factors to measure people on, such as personality, intelligence, individual motivation, skills and experience.' [1]

The problem for business is that making decisions based on flawed assumptions leads to mistakes. When hiring employees who are responsible for a business's social media, it is always far more effective to hire the most skilled person instead of basing your hiring decision on age.

Personal use vs business aptitude

Let's say someone is a great cook. They cook every day, love doing it and are extremely proficient in the kitchen. Could this skill easily translate into a successful business? Maybe. But there is a significant gap between the skills and knowledge it takes to be a great cook, and the skills and knowledge required to run a successful restaurant. Can the person prep and cook in volume? Can they adapt the food for people with allergies and different dietary requirements? Can they manage inventory and costs? What about hiring, managing and developing staff? Do they have the skills required for sales and customer service? Perhaps they can translate their personal aptitude into business success, but this shouldn't be assumed.

The same is true when translating any aptitude into business success. Social media is not an exception. Any technology can be used for different purposes and with varying degrees of effectiveness. Someone may be very comfortable working with computers and information technology, but be completely clueless when it comes to managing an Excel spreadsheet.

Others may use social media daily or even hourly for personal use. They may use several different platforms to communicate with friends and family, consume digital media and buy products online. This familiarity with social media may be an advantage that can translate into using social media for business purposes, but there is no guarantee their personal experience will directly translate into effective professional practice.

In some cases, people who are regular social media users and consumers may have picked up habits that are acceptable for personal social media use, but unacceptable for business purposes.

Separating the personal and workplace spheres

There's another interesting trend that suggests the increase in social media use for work may discourage the use of some social media. Recent research among younger people also shows there may be a backlash coming in younger users' perception of social media.

Research conducted by the Headmasters' and Headmistresses' Conference (HMC) and Digital Awareness UK found significant distrust of social media for personal use. Nearly two-thirds (63 per cent) of students said they would not care if social media did not exist, while 71 per cent reported taking long breaks or 'digital detoxes'. More than half reported experiencing abuse online.[2]

There may be more going on here. Now, many people are required to use social media for some or all their work. Some reports have suggested that using social media for work can discourage people from using social media for personal use – for example, one respondent to the HMC survey said:

> Because social media is my job I have to cut back, so I don't look at my Instagram after hours and I don't use Facebook unless I need to contact someone, or for work. I find this allows me to create clarity between my online and offline worlds. It's draining to be constantly connected, because sometimes I just want silence.'[3]

There is an interesting psychological concept at play here called the 'over-justification effect', which was initially described in 1971 by Edward Deci.[4] In the original experiments, participants were given games to play during the study, and were also allowed (but not required) to play the games while taking a break. Some participants were paid to play the game while others were not. Participants who were paid to play the game were far less likely to continue playing the game during their break than participants who were not paid until after the study was over.

The results demonstrate how paying people to complete an activity makes them less motivated to participate once the rewards are taken away. This is because there are two main types of motivation, which are quite distinctive:

- **Intrinsic motivators** motivate people to do work for some sort of internal reward. This can include things like a feeling of achievement at completing work that is challenging, recognition, being given responsibility, or the opportunity to do something meaningful. They bring satisfaction arising from the intrinsic conditions of the job itself.
- **Extrinsic motivators** are factors such as job security, salary, fringe benefits, work conditions, good pay, paid insurance and holidays. These tend not to give a strong sense of satisfaction, though dissatisfaction often results from their absence. These are outside of the value of the work itself, but are a key reward in most jobs.

Research has shown the over-justification effect arises consistently for all types of people, with different types of rewards and in different situations.[5,6] Essentially, paying people to do something makes them less likely to participate in that activity in the future if it does not come with a financial reward.

This is an important concept when discussing the overlap between social media managers' work and their personal lives. Although there may be some crossover in knowledge and experience, don't assume experience in using social media for personal communication will translate into expertise in its professional use. The two different domains may work happily in concert, but not always.

Social media policies and onboarding

Most workplaces have policies related to core activities and responsibilities at work. Companies have policies about recruitment and retention, use of business resources, bullying and sexual harassment, data protection, interactions with customers and a host of other domains. The same should be true about social media policy and digital communications (see Myth 14 for recommendations for social media policy).

Recruitment and onboarding is a good place to start. Employee orientation processes should introduce social media policies outlining guiding principles and general rules. If employees are allowed to use social media during work hours, it should cover the sort of use that is considered appropriate. For example, recruiters will likely spend a great deal of time on social media at work, but should probably not be posting political memes on the company accounts.

Development and training initiatives should assess social media competency, and work to build employee social media skills and understanding in a business context. For example, the style and content of work-related social media activity should be consistent with the company's objectives and values. This needs to be defined because social media activity will vary with company culture. Some companies may prefer more informal and light-hearted use of social media, while others will want to ensure employees are more professional and restrained.

Privacy and data protection policy must take social media use into account. Many companies have found, to their detriment, that the barrier between internal company information and its employees' social media use is rather too porous. Companies must ensure all employees understand what can and cannot be shared publicly on social media.

Conclusion

Never assume that any employee, irrespective of their age, knows everything about social media. Even for those recruits who have a great deal of experience with digital communication tools in a personal capacity, you cannot assume they understand all the etiquette and policy for social media use in a business context.

Notes

1 MacRae, I (2022) *Myths of Work: The stereotypes and assumptions holding your organization back*, Kogan Page, London

2 Parent/pupil digital behaviour poll – media briefing: www.hmc.org.uk/blog/parentpupil-digital-behaviour-poll-media-briefing/ (archived at https://perma.cc/JNW7-FWCB)

3 Why we millennials are so happy to be free of social media tyranny: www.theguardian.com/media/2017/nov/12/millennials-backlash-social-media-facebook-instagram-snapchat (archived at https://perma.cc/6HTL-E7AJ)

4 Deci, E L (1972) Effects of externally mediated rewards on intrinsic motivation, *Journal of Personality and Social Psychology*, **18** (**1**), pp 105–15

5 Tang, S and Hall, V C (1995) The over justification effect: A meta-analysis, *Applied Cognitive Psychology*, **9** (5), pp 365–404

6 Cerasoli, C P, Nicklin, J M and Ford, M T (2014) Intrinsic motivation and extrinsic incentives jointly predict performance: A 40-year meta-analysis, *Psychological Bulletin*, **140** (**4**), pp 980–1008

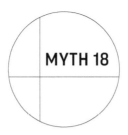

MYTH 18

Social media influencers are a new phenomenon

There is nothing new about celebrities setting or defining trends and then selling the associated products or services… Prominent and popular people who can reach an audience have always been paid to promote products or services.

Influencing people has always been more of an art than a science, so it is not especially easy to come up with clear metrics that define who is a successful 'influencer'. Someone could have millions of followers, but exert very little sway on their following (and may not even want to!), whereas a small circle of dedicated persuaders (often referred to as micro-influencers) can exert a great deal of influence.

It can be useful to look at the different kinds of influence exerted by people who create, develop, disseminate and endorse messages. In his 2000 book *The Tipping Point*, Malcom Gladwell talks about a relatively small group of socially savvy and skilled people who tend to have a significant influence.[1] Gladwell sorts these people into three different categories:

1 **Connectors** have wide communication networks and can influence many people. Gladwell explains these people in terms of traditional networks and direct interpersonal connections. However, it is easy to see how this idea is applicable to social media, where people can broadcast information to hundreds, thousands or even millions online.

2 **Mavens** are the specialists and experts who are the first to learn about new information, trends or ideas. They are knowledgeable, tend to be early adopters, and actively share their expertise or experience with others.

3 **Salespeople** are persuasive and charismatic and are good at convincing other people in their network. In 2000, Gladwell focused on the importance of non-verbal cues in convincing and persuading, but it is easy to see how this would be equally important on social media. Indeed, platforms like Instagram are designed to send messages using non-verbal cues and messages about someone's lifestyle, ideas and aspirations.

Influencer: a person with the ability to have an effect on others. They may be able to convince others to buy a specific product, adopt a certain idea or behave in a certain way by promotion or recommendation on social media.

The rise of the social influencer

From a traditional marketing perspective, influencer marketing has always existed. In the past it may have been referred to as 'partnership marketing' or 'relationship marketing', but the idea of connecting and aligning with a person or organization that has influence over a difficult-to-reach audience is not new. The technique has often been used to extend reach into a new territory or support one another as a joint venture and has been a mainstay of many marketing programmes, particularly in the business-to-business landscape. To that end, influencers come in many forms, from traditional, such as journalists, politicians, leaders, academics and subject matter experts, through to social media influencers. According to the Digital 2022 report, 22 per cent of social media users report 'following influencers' as one of the main reasons for using social media. As it's becoming ever more challenging for brands and organizations to cut through the content overwhelm and algorithm restrictions, it's this influencer audience that many brands and organizations have been tapping into.[2]

According to the 2022 Influencer Marketing Benchmark Report, influencer marketing is now valued at $16.4 billion, having grown significantly since 2016 when it was valued at $1.7 billion.[3] Successful influencers have turned a particular version of their life into a 'brand', but it's not always the case that bigger is better. In the Global Web Index Influencer Marketing Report, 56 per cent of influencer followers in the US and UK think influencers with up to 50,000 followers are the most credible, with 34 per cent of consumers saying they think influencers with a follower count between 1,000 and 10,000 are the most credible. And just 12 per cent of consumers think influencers with over a million followers are trustworthy.[4] So it's not the high-profile celebrity that's a hit with consumers, but rather the smaller, more trustworthy micro-influencers, or nano-influencers (many of whom don't even think of themselves as influencers). From a business perspective, these could be your employees or indeed your customers.

It would be extremely unwise to write off influencers on social media. Although there is a great deal of superficiality and silly antics, a lot of influencers are hard at work. On social media they are a dominant force in shaping culture, trends and consumer behaviour. When it is done in a well-organized and concerted way, social media influencers can generate a huge amount of buzz around a product or topic that seems organic. Social media platforms, for many people, are a casual and informal communication network. Trends that emerge can seem to appear from nowhere. When the top influencers all jump on a topic it can generate the feeling that 'everyone is talking about this'. In reality, it is more likely to be because one company is paying a lot of different influential people to talk about it.

As outlined in Myth 2, TikTok is a video-sharing social media application that took off in 2019. According to the *Wall Street Journal*, we can put TikTok's swift rise in 2019 down to a £776 million marketing budget from Chinese parent company Bytedance.[5] A concerted effort, bringing together tailored advertising and tapping into the massive networks of several influencers and content creators can provide an environment for a company's product to go viral. An unknown business can become a household name in a relatively short space of time if the marketing department is prepared to pay for it. Of course, for most organizations, brands and businesses, the more affordable option may be to tap into small micro-influencers, or leverage customers who are highly engaged with the brand, product or business and have a trusted network.

It is not only smaller businesses that leverage the micro-influencer market. Adidas chose to abandon the one-off celebrity influencer engagement in favour of a longer-term relationship with a team of the best street footballers. The company brought eight of these smaller aspirational micro-influencers together to create the first social media football team. They then chartered their journey over two seasons across Instagram, Facebook, YouTube and Twitter, driving millions of views and building a deeper connection with the influencers and the brand generally.[6]

Influencers are a growing force in advertising and the digital economy. Personal brands connected with specific styles, beliefs, ideologies and lifestyles are a natural partner for targeted advertising. If social media creates filter bubbles, influencers are the quickest way to get to the centre of any bubble.

Conclusion

There is nothing new about celebrities setting or defining trends and then selling the associated products or services. They may be on different platforms like YouTube and Instagram instead of on the radio and television, but the effect is largely the same. Prominent and popular people who can reach an audience have always been paid to promote products or services. Or, as in the case of joint ventures, partnership or relationship marketing, organizations have worked with those who are already influential in a particular market or audience sector, to extend reach and awareness.

Notes

1   Gladwell, M (2000) *The Tipping Point: How little things can make a big difference*, Little, Brown and Company, Boston, MA

2   Digital 2022 We Are Social Report: https://wearesocial.com/uk/blog/2022/01/digital-2022/ (archived at https://perma.cc/TD47-NYS6)

3   The state of influencer marketing 2022: Benchmark report: https://influencermarketinghub.com/influencer-marketing-benchmark-report/ (archived at https://perma.cc/DS5F-HZPG)

4   Influencer marketing: Exploring the current influencer marketing landscape and its future potential: https://www.gwi.com/hubfs/Downloads/Influencer_Marketing_report.pdf (archived at https://perma.cc/B67K-NUH7)

5   TikTok's videos are goofy. Its strategy to dominate social media is serious: www.wsj.com/articles/tiktoks-videos-are-goofy-its-strategy-to-dominate-social-media-is-serious-11561780861 (archived at https://perma.cc/ZFL7-73GN)

6   Influencer marketing: Exploring the current influencer marketing landscape and its future potential: https://www.gwi.com/hubfs/Downloads/Influencer_Marketing_report.pdf (archived at https://perma.cc/B67K-NUH7)

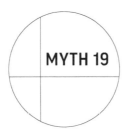

People have different personalities on social media

The way people think and behave on social media is influenced by their underlying, stable personality traits, and not the other way around.

To answer this myth we have to ask the question: are people fundamentally different online?

Social media websites have different cultures, norms and types of behaviour that are encouraged or discouraged (see Myth 25). If people act a bit differently depending which site they are on, social media must be changing people's personalities online, right? A *Forbes* article entitled 'Multiple personalities and social media: The many faces of me' makes that claim.[1] It suggests that people segment their personalities, and slot them into different online locations.

While it may be true that people tend to accentuate the positive, and omit some of the more mundane, uninteresting or unattractive parts of their lives and personalities on social media, this is no different to what people do in their everyday offline lives. Psychologists call it 'impression management'. It's a conscious or subconscious effort to present ourselves to other people in a certain light. The tools and techniques people use might be different in digital spaces compared with in physical spaces, but the core psychological processes are the same.

Social media may colour how people represent themselves, and highlight certain aspects of their personality and behaviour, but it doesn't change it. Some people have a jaundiced view of how people portray themselves on social media, while others may have rose-tinted spectacles. Yet all behaviour on social media gives us useful and measurable insight into a person's personality. Instead of obscuring or changing people's personality, social media allows us a better window into understanding how personality appears in different environments.

What is personality?

Personality is used to describe many different things, and on social media the term is used quite loosely. For example, 'personality quizzes' use a few light-hearted questions to provide a vague description of people – often matching them to characters from a movie or television series. In this broad sense, personality is used to refer to anything from character traits to motivation, values or ways of interacting with other people.

All references to 'personality' in this myth relate to the psychological definition of the term: 'a stable pattern of thinking, feeling and acting'.[2] The word 'stable' is important in this definition, because it means that an individual's personality remains more or less unchanged throughout their adult life.

The personality of a person is separable into specific and fundamental traits which exist on a continuum. Every person fits somewhere on that spectrum of personality, which is then relatable and understandable in the context of all other people. The combinations of personality traits can be unique, but the nature of personality means the model can be applied to everyone, irrespective of background, history, culture, experience, language or psychological states.

Personality traits are consistent, biologically hardwired and socially reinforced ways of thinking, feeling and behaving; this means they are unlikely to change very much from day to day or even year to year. They can shift over long periods of time with serious psychological intervention, but do not change in the same way that moods, relationships or a person's surroundings can. People may behave a bit differently in different situations – for example, they might act differently with their boss at work than with their colleagues in the pub, or talk in a different way in a Twitter direct message than with their grandmother. But these are minor changes in response to the environment, not radical shifts in personality. This holds just as true in cyberspace as it does in real-world situations.

Personality traits directly affect people's behaviour, their performance and relationships. They strongly influence people in all domains of their life: understanding themselves, the way they view other people and understand the world, set goals, communicate and organize their thoughts.

Measuring personality provides insight into how people operate, and can even be used to predict how successful they are likely to be at work.[3] Indeed, personality is one of the best predictors of workplace performance. Furthermore, someone's personality and behaviour online is a good indicator of how they will act outside of cyberspace.

Measuring and explaining personality

There are six separable personality traits, as shown in the box, which can be measured on a continuum. Certain traits will be a better fit to some workplace roles and cultures than others. It's even possible to pinpoint optimal levels of traits for certain roles and workplaces. We can look at desirable workplace criteria and the functionality of certain traits using tools like the High Potential Traits Indicator.[2,3]

THE SIX PERSONALITY TRAITS

1 **Conscientiousness**. Self-motivation, long-term planning and achievement orientation.
2 **Adjustment**. Capacity to manage stress effectively with a lower level of emotional reactivity.

---

3 **Curiosity**. Openness to new experiences, ideas and processes with excitement about learning new things.

4 **Ambiguity Acceptance**. Capacity to manage complexity, mixed messages and thrive when processes or outcomes are uncertain.

5 **Risk Approach**. A proactive approach to managing personal and interpersonal challenges.

6 **Competitiveness**. A focus on outcomes, receiving rewards for achievements and a desire to win.

There is another perspective from which to view personality traits: the 'dark side'. This involves understanding what happens when things go wrong, and the counterproductive or even destructive behaviours that can emerge under extreme stress, challenge or adversity. When we look at personality styles, we can see the default beliefs people have about themselves and the world, and the behaviours they tend to rely on to manage their goals, social relationships and stress. There are three different categories that are particularly useful in understanding people's chosen strategies for dealing with conflict on social media:

Cluster A: Eccentric styles

People who score high in these styles tend to set themselves apart from others or from groups using caution, independence or eccentricity. Under stress or threat, they tend to distance themselves from others. Their key 'dark side' traits are as follows:

- Wary – cautious and suspicious about the motivations of other people and tend to be hypervigilant. They are good at threat detection.
- Solitary – prefer to work alone, often in highly specialized occupations. They are good at independent work and thought.
- Unconventional – need to be seen as unique and different. They dislike 'normal' and are good at approaching problems from a different perspective.

For people who use these styles, learning to navigate complex organizational and social structures may be more challenging because they tend to disengage.

Cluster B: Assertive styles

Individuals who use these styles to cope with adversity tend to be very active in establishing new connections and moving between positions and relationships. Under stress, they tend to look for other people to blame. Their key 'dark side' traits are as follows:

- Aggressive – have a persistent desire for thrill-seeking. They are good at taking decisive action.
- Impulsive – highly emotionally reactive. They are good at initiating relationships and sparking new ideas.
- Dramatic – need to be the centre of attention. They are good at commanding and holding the attention of others.

- Confident – presentation and image are extremely important to them. They are good at impression management.
- Resourceful – value outcomes over relationships. They are good at getting things done at all costs.

People who use these styles tend to be the quickest to adapt to new social environments. They are more likely to take advantage of situations where there is less structure and oversight with more opportunity for risk and complexity. This can either create new opportunities or get them into trouble quickly.

Cluster C: Anxious styles

People who use these styles tend to prefer collaboration to competition and prioritize the development of positive relationships with colleagues. Under stress, they tend to blame themselves and seek the approval of colleagues they look up to. Their key 'dark side' traits are as follows:

- Sensitive – keenly aware of interpersonal conflicts. They are good at peace-making and consensus-building.
- Selfless – have a strong need to be useful and helpful to others. They are good at advisory and support roles.
- Perfectionistic – high desire for order, control and productivity. They are good at long-term planning.

Often people who report high levels of these personality styles like to have a clear organizational structure. They work most effectively when they feel safe, secure and supported and desire a strong sense of belonging within a team or company.

> **Go further**: Go online to highpotentialpsych.co.uk, take the test and see where you score on the dark-side personality styles, and how your results compare to other people.

Behaviour on social media

People's personalities are quite stable over time. Personality impacts how people assess and understand different situations and environments, which is why people tend to behave very similarly and in a predictable way when they are working on similar tasks.

Researchers have found that people's behaviour on social media closely aligns with their personality traits. The same traits that are influencing their behaviour in the real world are influencing their behaviour in these digital spaces.[4] The nature of social media actually makes this relatively easy to test, because many people post a huge amount of personal information, photos and social interaction online.

Conclusion

This is one myth that is relatively easy to dispel, because there is a substantial amount of research with clear conclusions. Personality traits are stable, measurable, and are directly linked to behaviour in predictable patterns both online and offline.

Notes

1 Multiple personalities and social media: The many faces of me: www. forbes.com/sites/meghancasserly/2011/01/26/multiple-personalities-and-social-media-the-many-faces-of-me (archived at https://perma.cc/ 9TVT-H9YB)

2 MacRae, I and Furnham, A (2018) *High Potential: How to spot, manage and develop talented people at work*, Bloomsbury, London

3 Robson, D (2018) The secrets of the 'high potential' personality: https:// www.bbc.com/worklife/article/20180508-the-secrets-of-the-high-potential-personality (archived at https://perma.cc/C4VF-UA9E)

4 Azucar, D, Marengo, D and Settanni, M (2018) Predicting the Big 5 personality traits from digital footprints on social media: A meta-analysis, *Personality and Individual Differences*, **124**, pp 150–59

MYTH 20

Saying the wrong thing on social media will get me cancelled

There are very few people who are personally equipped to deal with a barrage of personal abuse and threats in any environment, and even fewer who have the psychological and social supports to manage a professional response to them in the moment.

While some commentators, politicians and public figures seem to revel in controversy, deliberately riling up social media mobs to attract attention, most people don't want to be loathed online. Most people struggle with the complexities and anxieties that come with interpersonal conflict within their immediate circle of friends, family and colleagues. Only small percentage of people with certain personality disorders are immune to the stressors that come from interpersonal conflict[1] (see Myth 19).

Most adults have only three or four very close friends, with a wider network of friends, colleagues and acquaintances. The scale of social contact and connection online can be staggering in contrast to smaller, more intimate friendship groups within physical space. Much of digital interaction is simplified and codified in easily quantifiable ways. That's part of the genius of how social media companies have condensed social interactions at a global scale: it's difficult to conceptualize the responses of thousands of people to a post, but easier to understand when it's neatly summed up as a few thousand 'likes' or even millions of 'views'.

But we can't process that scale of a social reaction in the same way: our brains are not wired to cope with thousands or even millions of people giving social information and communication all at the same time. When that social information is aggressive, threatening or hateful, very few people are capable of managing their response.

The fear and risk of getting cancelled

A lot of people are understandably fearful about being on the receiving end of a social media mob. The difference between a smattering of online criticism and a full-on pile on from a swelling mob is considerable. It's staggering how a social media mob can get out their virtual torches and pitchforks with the aim of destroying their target psychologically and socially, not to mention professionally. Social media mobs can be vicious, antisocial and unconscionable.

This is a legitimate concern. Being on the receiving end of such a mob is known as getting 'cancelled'. It's effectively cyberbullying. No book can guarantee how other people will respond to your behaviour online, but it is worth discussing the potential risks and social anxiety that people can experience.

To cancel (on social media):

1 To cancel someone (usually a celebrity or other well-known figure) means to stop giving support to that person. The act of cancelling could entail boycotting an actor's movies or no longer reading or promoting a writer's works.

2 The act of using mob pressure to harass or 'expose' someone online for any past or present drama, no matter how insignificant it may be.[2]

The experience of 'getting cancelled'

We spoke to Chris Boutté, who was on the receiving end of a social media firestorm, and got 'cancelled' in 2019.

Chris ran a mental health discussion channel on social media (The Rewired Soul) which was increasing in popularity. He led mental health discussions among Facebook and Discord communities and posted a substantial amount of content on a variety of channels with an engaged and expanding audience on YouTube. He is still active on social media and his podcast *The Rewired Soul* has taken a significantly different focus, with more emphasis on conversations with experts.

Chris's style and approach is very well suited to YouTube: he's vibrant, expressive and extraordinarily open about his own experience and history of mental health. He brings this perspective into the topics he covers, but, in his own words, he 'can be blunt [...], petty and sometimes passive aggressive'.[3] While his style appeals to many, he can also rub some people up the wrong way.

Before refocusing his podcast he covered a range of topics that typically generate a lot of interest on social media: mental health and well-being, current events, drugs, addiction, pop culture and celebrities (both old-school and social media stars) to name a few. All these topics were accompanied by a large dose of social commentary. Chris isn't a psychologist, nor does he claim to be.

Chris often waded into one topic that receives a lot of attention on YouTube and pop culture in general: the psychology and mental health of celebrities. This topic can be controversial. The efficacy and validity of discussing the psychological states and traits of public figures as a learning tool is hotly debated by psychologists as well as social commentators. It is complicated by the fact that many public figures start public conversations about their own psychological traits and states.

Chris discusses his own experiences, and the value of having other people to talk to in mental health support, particularly in the sphere of recovery from addiction: 'My channel was all about mental health and addiction recovery. I'm not a therapist, I got sober through a 12-step programme. I just needed people who understood what I was going through.'

Chris is very clear about his approach to social media and his digital brand: part of his brand is both open discussion, and insight from his personal experience. He is happy to offer his opinion about almost any topic. He also draws a clear distinction between his own personal social media presence and a corporate brand: 'My brand is very different from someone who might who work on Wall Street or an investment banker. They don't necessarily need to post their opinions. But we live in a day and time where everyone wants to be the next social media star, so it's hard to rein it in.'

As Chris's social media prominence rose, his discussions about the mental health of public figures eventually generated a huge backlash in 2019. Figure 20.1 shows the intense spike of interest that the controversy provoked. The online anger wasn't just academic discussions or constructive criticism. Parts of the social media mob were making vicious and violent threats. Chris and his family received messages containing threats of physical violence and personal and professional destruction.

There are very few people who are personally equipped to deal with a barrage of personal abuse and threats in any environment, and even fewer who have the psychological and social supports to manage a response to them in the moment. Most people respond poorly when in extreme states of stress because the physiological and psychological reaction to stress restricts us both physically and mentally.

FIGURE 20.1 Frequency of Google searches for *The Rewired Soul* over time

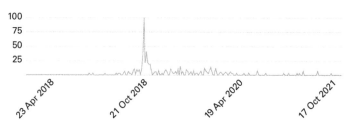

People in extreme states of stress have a diminished capacity to see alternatives, and look to eliminate that stress with less awareness or concern about secondary consequences. Our fight or flight impulses take over, and do whatever our experience has taught us will get us out of the imminent danger most quickly. There's a certain amount of training and preparation that can mitigate these effects, but the more novel the situation, the more difficult it is to prepare for.

Chris talks about how he responded to such extreme levels of stress. It erupted when he was travelling for work:

> I had no impulse control; it's one of the reasons I want people to start pausing more. I started doing a livestream in the airport, waiting for my connecting flight, trying to address some things. That didn't help. I couldn't focus on the conference; I would try to run back to my hotel room to make videos. One particular time I made a video around midnight – which went terribly as well. I made mistake after mistake after mistake. But we all have this urge to defend ourselves.

Chris said that in situations like the one he found himself in, it doesn't matter how many points you try to address or rebut, there will always be more. There are so many people with different motivations that it's impossible to argue individual points. No one will be satisfied with the responses, and all responding does is add fuel to the fire, creating more content for other people to criticize. Psychologically, Chris was at breaking point and struggling to cope with the onslaught of messages: 'At one point I broke down crying in the airport. My girlfriend and my mom were worried that I was going to relapse – and that idea came up a million times.'

Caught up in the heat of the moment, it can feel impossible to separate who you really are from the person strangers are telling you that you are:

> When you have hundreds of thousands of strangers telling you that you are a terrible person, it really messes with you. It's easier when one random person on Twitter comes after you, but when you have thousands of people coming after you, it feels like we're not evolutionarily wired for that. When you have that many people screaming at you, you start to think: damn, am I a terrible person?

Chris still seems to be processing the experience and working on what both he and other people can learn from it. For him, one of the biggest difficulties was the public aggression that came from people he had known for a long time. They discounted their own experiences they had had with him, opting instead to join in with the mob: 'the most difficult part for me, personally, was people who knew me and people who I had helped.'

Avoiding getting cancelled

This myth, and indeed this book, is not going to provide a detailed guide to what topics are 'safe' for social media, which topics will not court controversy or backlash, and what should be verboten. It would be an exercise in futility that would be out of date before the book is published. What we can do is relate this story back to the core advice of this book: understand your content and your audience, and have a deliberate strategy for your social media activity. As Chris advises, reflect on the motives behind your behaviour. Even when your brand is about openness and authenticity, sometimes it is best to err on the side of discretion: 'Check your motives: am I just doing something to signal to other people what a good person I am, because if that's my motive then I'll just shut my (stupid) face.'

Alongside that, there are a few pieces of advice for corporate social media use in Myth 14, and business leaders and people with a larger digital presence can learn from the advice in Myth 22, with practical tips for leaders on social media.

Conclusion

This is not a myth. Saying the wrong thing on social media can get you cancelled, and it can be an incredibly damaging experience personally, psychologically as well as professionally. There is no moderator, no independent support, and no external organization that can effectively regulate or enforce standards of behaviour or civility on the actions of a social media mob. There are steps you can take to avoid controversial topics: ensure your content is focused, professional and is well researched. If you understand your audience and your content and follow a deliberate strategy instead of reacting to topical and controversial topics, you'll be much better able to manage and predict the responses you receive on social media.

Notes

1   MacRae, I (2021) *Dark Social: Understanding the darker side of work, personality and social media*, Bloomsbury, London
2   Urban dictionary: https://www.urbandictionary.com/define. php?term=Canceled (archived at https://perma.cc/XMJ3-QT6Z)
3   Boutté, C (2021) Pride: How cancel culture broke me: https://www. therewiredsoul.com/blog/cancel-culture-broke-me (archived at https:// perma.cc/UE5E-YD44)

MYTH 21

Public social media profiles are fair game for employers and recruiters

Companies that abuse their access to personal data will make people more cautious about sharing it in the future. This has the potential to make it more challenging for everyone, even those businesses that operate ethically and legally.

There is a wealth of information available online about both people and businesses. While a small minority of people don't engage with social media, around 72 per cent of people and 84 per cent of 18–29-year-olds have social media profiles.[1] The amount of information people share publicly varies wildly, but many social media users still seem unaware how easily and often content that is not intended to become public, becomes very public.

Anyone who uses the internet is constantly sharing information. Chatting, emailing, researching, shopping, ordering taxis and takeaways, reading the news and posting photos are all ways in which a person's everyday life is recorded and stored. In Myth 29, we detail exactly how much information is held about just one person (in this case, one of the authors). But social media companies dwarf most other online organizations by the sheer volume of personal data they collect. Much of it is securely recorded and stored. But as a general rule, remember anything that is shared digitally can easily become public.

Any person or organization can access information that people post on social media – platforms like Twitter, Facebook, Instagram and others are a treasure trove of trends, public opinion and potential customer data. The legal and ethical rules around using this data exist, but are often ignored. Because technology develops at a much more rapid pace than public policy or legislation, there are some large grey areas concerning how much information companies should collect (and do collect) about people.

For the sake of simplicity and clarity, this myth focuses on using people's personal data in the workplace, particularly in relation to recruitment.

Data collection for employee selection

Are public social media profiles fair game for recruiters and hiring managers? Can employers search social media pages and the web for information about potential job candidates? Legally, this is a grey area that varies between countries. In regions that fall under the European Union's General Data Protection Regulation (GDPR) legislation, and countries that have adopted these rules like the United Kingdom (see Myths 7 and 29), there are restrictions on what information employers can access and for what purpose. However, the rules are far more flexible and less weighted towards protecting the data of individuals outside of Europe.

Some social media profiles are deliberately set up for people to broadcast their information to recruiters, hiring managers and other professional audiences. LinkedIn and job search websites are good examples of this. Social media platforms that are set up to share work-related information such as work history, education and past employment experience are often intended to be seen by employers.

Screening employees on social media

Most employers check prospective job candidates online before they hire them. In 2018, a YouGov poll found that 80 per cent of employers have used, or would use, online social media profiles to screen potential hires.[2]

Although precise and reliable figures aren't readily available, it's clear that social media screening is a common practice by recruiters and employers – and anyone on the job hunt should be aware of this. Larger companies are more likely to check candidates' social media profiles, and are also more likely to filter out candidates based on what they see on social media. According to a YouGov survey, while only 11 per cent of small companies had turned down candidates after checking up on their social media, 28 per cent of larger companies had done the same.[3]

Before discussing the pros and cons of taking this approach, there is one significant elephant in the room – legality. In the United States, it is legal to view any material that job candidates have posted publicly, whereas in the European Union it is not. Any area that falls under the GDPR requires that businesses obtain informed consent prior to accessing, storing or using someone's personal data.

This means that job candidates must give the prospective employer 'informed consent' before that company can review any personal data that may be available on social media and use this in evaluating their suitability for a job – even when this information is already publicly available. Best practice should involve telling prospective job candidates exactly what you are looking for, what information you might use, and how the hiring decision will be made. That includes any background checks or reviews of information you might find about them online.

Another legal risk of using social media in job screening is that many sites include information, attitudes and opinions that are not directly related to the job. Employment law in most countries requires that employees be evaluated only on factors that are directly related to the job (called a bona fide occupational qualification). Yet social media sites may contain a lot of additional information, from political and religious beliefs to everyday behaviours, that is irrelevant to the job but influences judgements about the job candidate.

Some of the most common red flags identified by recruiters on social media sites are not legal to use in hiring decisions. Twenty-nine per cent of business decision makers say online political views/activity would stop someone getting hired (definitely not legal), and 26 per cent said that having too many photos of themselves on a social media profile could be disqualifying (certainly not a bona fide occupational qualification).[3]

In the 2000s and early 2010s, when some companies were far more tech-savvy than legislators, there was a lot more legal wriggle room to use social media profiles in the job screening process. Now that legislation is trying to catch up to the technology, employers must be more cautious about using social media data in the selection process. If you are going to use social media profiles to screen job candidates, here are some guidelines:

- The guidelines on discrimination and fair hiring practice all apply to social media in the candidate screening process.
- Only data that is relevant to the role can and should be evaluated in the screening process. This includes qualifications, experience, education and factors directly relevant to the job.
- Any personal data collected should be absolutely necessary to the hiring process, and no excessive or irrelevant data should be collected (this can be very challenging to disaggregate from a personal social media profile).
- Social media searches should look for specific, predefined information or criteria and not be a general trawling exercise.
- Reasonable steps should be taken to verify the accuracy of any information.
- Distinguish between social media used for personal and professional purposes. For example, a LinkedIn profile

is typically used for professional purposes, while Facebook is typically used for personal purposes.

- Professional information in the public domain can be used. For example, work they have published, information from professional or trade bodies, and information published from past employers on a public website or social media platform.
- Applicants must be advised of the screening beforehand and provide informed consent for their personal information to be used.
- Applicants should receive the opportunity to respond to any negative or adverse findings that arise from a social media search, and their response should be considered in the decision-making process.

Data harvesting changes behaviour

As social media becomes increasingly common and accessible, people are becoming more restrictive in their privacy settings.[4] The more information that people post publicly on social media, the more individuals, organizations and computer programs will comb through that data for their own purposes. This understandably has a chilling effect on people's willingness to share their data publicly.

Highly effective analytics can be a victim of their own success. Once people's data can be analysed to make predictions about factors such as personality and behaviour (especially commercial behaviour), many people will become more wary about sharing their information. There is good evidence to suggest that social media companies and even search engines can go beyond just predicting behaviour to influencing it, in everything from shopping decisions to seeking mental health support.[5,6]

The battle between privacy and access to information online will continue to be a dynamic process for both users and those who employ analytics, as people's behaviour and approach to social media adapt to a continually evolving landscape. It also means that companies will continue to adapt with social media, its users and in the regulatory landscape.

Conclusion

Laws around accessing prospective and current employees' social media profiles are continually tightening. As the law catches up with the tech, employers should make sure they are sticking to the rules – they can no longer assume that public social media profiles are fair game. Companies that abuse their access to personal data will make people more cautious about sharing it in the future. This has the potential to make it more challenging for everyone, even those businesses that operate ethically and legally.

Notes

1   Social media fact sheet: www.pewresearch.org/internet/fact-sheet/
    social-media/ (archived at https://perma.cc/Q3VG-YVTV)
2   YouGov survey results: https://d25d2506sfb94s.cloudfront.net/cumulus_
    uploads/document/wkikbhg88s/InternalResults_170316_business_
    decision_makers.pdf (archived at https://perma.cc/RX4C-M9EU)

3 Disgracebook: One in five employers have turned down a candidate because of social media: https://yougov.co.uk/topics/politics/articles-reports/2017/04/10/disgracebook-one-five-employers-have-turned-down-c (archived at https://perma.cc/W9B5-CSMC)

4 MacRae, I, and Furnham, A (2018) *High Potential: How to spot, manage and develop talented people at work*, Bloomsbury, London

5 I used Google Ads for social engineering It worked: www.nytimes.com/2019/07/07/opinion/google-ads.html (archived at https://perma.cc/ZRX5-5ALT)

6 Preoţiuc-Pietro, D et al (2015) Studying user income through language, behaviour and affect in social media, *PLoS ONE*, **10** (9)

MYTH 22

Business leaders don't need a presence on social media

Given the transparency, connectivity and reach of social media platforms, both externally and internally, social media presents the perfect opportunity for leaders to connect and communicate with people on a frequent basis.

Digital and social media leadership in business is no longer a fresh concept. In a world where most people are now engaged with social media, most key stakeholders (be that employees, customers, investors and indeed competitors) use social media to stay informed. Brunswick Group's 2021 Connected Leadership report cites that 74 per cent of people want leaders and senior executives to speak openly through these platforms and expect business leaders to use social media to communicate with the public.[1] Employees not only expect business leaders to use social media to communicate, they would prefer by more than a 5:1 ratio to work for a CEO who uses social media compared to a CEO who does not. Unfortunately, despite these growing employee and customer expectations, the Connected Leadership report cites that only 51 per cent of employees say their company leaders are using social media to reach them and their co-workers. When you consider the numerous opportunities social media brings, such as brand building, business development and thought leadership, this is a considerable oversight.

In this myth, we'll explore the benefits of leaders having a presence on social media, and the practicalities of ensuring that presence is authentic and drives trust and engagement.

Let's talk about trust

In 2022, The Edelman Trust Barometer reported that business is now the most trusted organization, with trust in government and media tumbling. Trust in business has even surpassed trust in NGOs. People want more, not less, business engagement on societal issues, and believe business can solve more ills than governments. When it comes to communication, 78 per cent of people believe CEOs should be personally visible, and 56 per cent of employees expect CEOs to speak publicly about controversial social and political issues they care about.[2]

It's clear from the research and customer and employee sentiment that there's a growing need for leaders within businesses to be visible and communicate openly with their key stakeholders. Given the transparency, connectivity and reach of social media platforms, both externally and internally (using networks such as Slack, Workplace, WhatsApp and Yammer) social media presents the perfect opportunity for leaders to connect and communicate with people on a frequent basis.

What's stopping leaders taking to social?

Previous research we have undertaken in this space has highlighted four key aspects that prevent CEOs and leaders getting on board with social media and using it as part of their day-to-day role:

- Lack of experience – leaders may be unsure how to utilize the technologies, what to say, and how to communicate it.
- Time – leaders may not have enough time to include social media in their daily routine.
- ROI – leaders may find it difficult to justify the effort/ reward and actual return on investment.
- Fear – leaders may be fearful of making a fool of themselves, losing face, saying the incorrect thing, or of no one participating.

A detailed account of this research is published in *Get Social: Social media strategy and tactics for leaders*.[3]

First impressions count

There is evidence that things may be changing, particularly in the wake of the Covid-19 pandemic. Given the escalation of digital transformation programmes, and the wider engagement of social media technologies during and following the pandemic, many more leadership teams and organizations have become far more familiar and adept with both internal and external social platforms. This a good thing, as clearly many stakeholders turn to social media to find out more about leaders. The Connected Leadership 2021 research report showcases that stakeholders will draw their first impressions of leaders – and often companies – from digital sources, citing the following statistics:

- 49 per cent use the corporate website
- 45 per cent look at the CEO's LinkedIn page
- 44 per cent search results on Google for the CEO
- 41 per cent use the CEO's Facebook account
- 39 per cent use the CEO's Twitter account
- 37 per cent look at the CEO's blog
- 35 per cent view the CEO's Instagram account
- 34 per cent search the CEO's Wikipedia entry
- 25 per cent listen to the CEO's podcast
- 21 per cent read reviews of the CEO on Glassdoor
- 19 per cent view discussion about the CEO on Reddit.[4]

So, given the pace of change, and indeed the remote working landscape we find ourselves amidst, are you or your leadership team giving enough consideration to your online presence? It's important that the first impression given by any of the sources cited in the above list is a favourable one. According to the 2021 Connected Leadership report, if organizations want to connect employees to a shared purpose and vision, then leadership must adapt to connect across the entire workforce through digital and social media.

Social CEO exemplars

There are many great examples of CEOs and leaders who have taken the time to understand the nuances of social media platforms. They have made the platforms firmly part of their everyday interactions and key tools for both insight and communication. Damian Corbet's book, *The Social CEO*, includes chapters from 27 leaders, across a range of industry sectors, who have embraced social technologies to support their work, employee engagement, network development and thought leadership. Damian concludes:

> Transparent. Open. Honest. Engaged. Community-minded. These are qualities that today's social CEOs hold close to their hearts. They live and work in the open; they engage with their communities – internally and externally; they share their ideas and values: they admit their mistakes. It's hard to imagine CEOs twenty or thirty years ago behaving like this; they'd probably have been laughed out of the boardroom.[5]

Indeed, findings from research and interviews with CEOs and leaders we published in *Get Social* identified individuals such as John Legere, former CEO of T-Mobile. John is now retired and still highly visible on social media. He advised that, for him, social media is the most important tool in the CEO's modern-day toolbox. He shared that listening in via social media, in real time, to better understand not only what his competitors were doing, but what his employees and customers were saying and feeling, was critical to product and service innovation. It also helped him to be a more informed and engaged leader. He often spoke directly with employees on social media, many of whom were in a different geographical location and would not have had access to him otherwise.

Indeed, in all the many interviews we conducted, listening on social media was deemed one of the most useful aspects of engaging with the platforms. And while it was acknowledged that CEOs listening in via social media wasn't necessarily statistically conclusive, the insights were typically directionally accurate. As Brian J Dunn, former CEO of Best Buy, shared, it's 'a great way to take the consumers' temperature on any given topic relating to your business and an interesting data point on your competitors.'

The practicalities of being a social CEO

As outlined in the books we referenced, here are five practical lessons to help leaders get started with social media:

- Listen: This aspect is so important, it's worth mentioning again. As former CEO Brian J Dunn told us; 'Listening in helps me to see round corners'. Whether you're using sophisticated social listening software, such as Brandwatch, and reviewing the insights, or you're just staying tuned in to the regular drumbeat across the channels you tune into, listening is a critical component of any conversation.

- Channel selection: Choose the channel, or channels, that naturally fit(s) with the leaders. If they like Instagram and find it easy to navigate, then perhaps stick to one channel – or perhaps a blend of LinkedIn and Twitter. Get comfortable with the nuances and decide what works. No one expects leaders to spend all their time mastering social media, but having a presence that allows people to access them and get to know, like and trust them, is now an expectation.

- Keep it real: Social media activity is conversational. Anything too polished or orchestrated by the PR team will be evident. Of course, as a leader you'll need to be considered about your position but see it as an opportunity to share your voice in a way you would ordinarily do in a meeting. Be professional but human.

- Work as a team: From a leadership perspective, social media is not your main role. It's a communication channel that enables you to tune in and stay abreast of key stakeholder views and the landscape you operate in. It allows you to communicate as and when you want and need to. You can support your team with the insights and content development and perhaps even scheduling. It's likely there is a team or person responsible for social media communications within your organization, so tap into the resources you have. It can be a good opportunity for reverse mentoring.

- Build a strategy: Perfection often hampers progress, but from a CEO or senior leadership perspective, you want to ensure that the role you occupy on social media mirrors the role you occupy at the helm of the business. Yes, be human, but also ensure that you have a clear understanding of what you are doing, and what you want to be known for and seen as, supporting your content creation, voice and objectives.

Conclusion

The leadership landscape has changed significantly. As evidenced in this myth there are many positive aspects associated with leaders utilizing social media, from sourcing insights to engagement and speaking out on societal issues. Importantly, it helps leaders to stay current and close to key stakeholders. Leadership needs a presence on social media.

Notes

1 Brunswick Consulting (2021) Connected Leadership Report, https://www.brunswickgroup.com/media/8059/connected-leadership-2021-report.pdf (archived at https://perma.cc/VC5M-EDTH)

2 Edelman Trust Barometer 2022, https://www.edelman.co.uk/sites/g/files/aatuss301/files/2022-01/2022%20Edelman%20Trust%20Barometer_UK.pdf? (archived at https://perma.cc/WH8V-ES6R)

3 Carvill, M (2018) *Get Social: Social media strategy and tactics for leaders*, Kogan Page, London

4   Brunswick Consulting (2021) Connected Leadership Report, https://
    www.brunswickgroup.com/media/8059/connected-leadership-2021-
    report.pdf (archived at https://perma.cc/J9DN-T9Z6)
5   Corbet, D (2019) *The Social CEO: How social media can make you a
    stronger leader*, Bloomsbury, London

Social media is full of #fakenews

Misinformation, parody and satire exist, as they always have, in different mediums and formats. It's essential to use trusted sources, critical thinking and to be a cautious consumer of media, irrespective of the platform.

'Fake news' made its first appearance on *Dictionary.com* in 2017, but it is hardly a novel concept. Concern about misinformation in media, and politicians and public figures disliking media coverage is nothing new. Consider the US President who said, 'There has been more new error propagated by the press in the last ten years than in a hundred years before.' That was John Adams, in 1798.[1]

Although fake news and misinformation may be widespread on social media, it is hard to know whether it is any different to before, or more pernicious. Research by Lazer and colleagues in 2018, published in *Science*, suggested that there is still limited understanding and research around the scale and effect of fake news.[2] They suggest that rigorous research still needs to be conducted to understand how much fake news is out there, the effects it really has on people, and how individuals and social media platforms filter information.

Fake news: False news stories, often of a sensational nature, created to be widely shared or distributed for the purpose of generating revenue, or promoting or discrediting a public figure, political movement, company, etc.

The accusation that information on social media can be distorted, biased or massaged is certainly true. Similar accusations have been hurled at newspapers, books, pamphlets and any other medium used for communicating information. In 17th-century Britain, King Charles II issued 'A Proclamation to restrain the Spreading of False News', meaning information that the king worried was helping 'to nourish an universal jealousy and dissatisfaction in the minds of all His Majesties good subjects'. It stopped short of complaining about Crooked Cromwell – very unfair!

Different types of fake news

When looking at the veracity of news and information on social media, you'll probably notice that there are grey areas. This is how we categorize and define how we see these: there are truths that can be objectively proved; there are statements that are true for a particular person; there are outright falsehoods; then there are exaggerated lies. For example:

1 Ben Nevis is the tallest mountain in the UK.
2 Mount Snowdon is the tallest mountain I've ever seen in the UK!
3 Mount Snowdon is huge; it must be the biggest in the UK.
4 Mount Snowdon is the tallest mountain in the world!

The first is objectively true and easily verifiable. The second could certainly be accurate for one person or many people. Then, it's a slippery slope down to the third and fourth statements. But it is incredibly useful to distinguish between objective facts, people's observations and blatant lies.

Tandoc and colleagues[3] identify six types of 'fake' news which vary widely in purpose, context and audience. The first three types are satire, parody and fabrication. We discuss these in detail below as they are closely aligned with common usages of the term 'fake news'. We cover the final three types – photo manipulation, PR and propaganda – more briefly, as they are further from the common usage.

News satire

News satire is one of the most common types of 'fake news' in the research literature. This uses a humorous and often exaggerated approach, presenting information in the format of a typical news broadcast. There are plenty of examples of these with a long history, with shows such as *Have I Got*

News For You in the UK and *Saturday Night Live's Weekend Update* in the US. Satire presents news that is deliberately distorted for comedic purposes. It often presents stories that sound as if they could be true, but are not.

However, there is a trend towards satire becoming a staple of mainstream media as a method of presenting criticism, shaping political opinions and affecting discourse, and this inevitably filters through to social media. This is not a completely new idea: the ancient Greeks wrote plays that satirized the forms of government of the neighbouring city-states, and in 1729 Jonathan Swift's *A Modest Proposal* satirically (and elaborately) explained how the solution to famine in Ireland was to eat babies. Satire is often an effective form of rhetoric that resonates with people.

Satirical sites on social media also blur the lines between humour, news and trolling: RAF Luton on Twitter is a great example of a hilarious and satirical profile of an (imaginary) Royal Air Force base that often draws irritation and anger from uncritical social media users who react with outrage before checking the source.

News fabrication

News fabrication is a style of manufacturing false information but presenting it as truth. This is more pernicious because it is deliberately designed to misrepresent facts and to misinform the audience. The format is fundamentally different from parody and satire because of the relationship between the presenter of the information and the reader or viewer. In the comedic presentation of parody or satire, there is an understanding that the consumer is not meant to take the information entirely seriously.

Tandoc and colleagues explain that news fabrication makes use of partial truths, deliberately misinterpreting facts and drawing on audience biases to create a narrative that is presented as factual. These often have a bias from either side of the political spectrum, for example the right-wing site *Breitbart*, or the *Canary* on the left. Often news fabrication combines a variety of factual (or at least plausible) sources of information to manufacture misinformation. Some of these sites mix 'fake' news with plausible or verifiable stories – so although certain sources can sometimes be reliable, they need to be treated very sceptically.

News fabrication sites also form a core part of larger disinformation ecosystems. These can be part of deliberate, state-backed groups that generate fabricated news on fringe sites or social media channels that are deliberately engineered to be picked up on more mainstream news, social media channels, or other state-backed media organizations. Sometimes these stories get picked up and referenced by a set of channels, each new citation adding some perceived legitimacy to fabricated information.[4]

News parody

News parody is another humorous interpretation of a mainstream news format, but it often deliberately uses false information for comedic effect. This format has flourished online with publications like the *Onion* or the *Beaverton*, which present fake stories with a sly wink. The stories are intended to be deliberately outrageous or surprising. While the information is presented seriously, there is an understanding that the content is completely fabricated for comedic purposes.

The distinction between news parody and news fabrication or the spread of fake news is not always clear-cut. These satirical stories can get picked up by more legitimate news sources when writers don't check their facts or sources, and the lines of parody and satire start to blur. For example, when news parody website *World Daily News Report* reported a fabricated story that drag queen RuPaul had been groped by Donald Trump in the 1990s, the story quickly spread across tabloids and social media.

The next three categories are also familiar ways of massaging the truth or distorting information, but may not be what most people think of as 'fake news'.

Photo manipulation

This is a way of misrepresenting visual instead of written information. It is common practice, and widely recognized, that images are often touched up, changed, edited or modified from the original. Photo manipulation has become more common in relation to news fabrication. For example, images can be combined, modified and edited to include a logo from a news website to fabricate images that are presented as real.

Advertising and PR

In the context of fake news, this describes promotional material passed off as news for financial gain. This occurs when advertising is presented as a news report, or a press release is published as news. The distortion is 'when public relations practitioners adopt the practices and/or appearance of journalists in order to insert marketing or other persuasive messages into news media'.[5]

This is very prevalent online in the form of paid marketing content which does not give any indication to the reader that it is actually an advertisement.

Propaganda

Propaganda is not new, but there has been a re-emergence of interest in information that is distorted for political purposes. These stories are usually misrepresentations of facts, presented as news but designed to benefit a political leader, group or organization. For example, research on Channel One in Russia shows long-term patterns of a media company that presents itself as news, but is used to distribute 'strategic narratives' and shape political narratives, with little regard to facts or evidence.

The final definition of fake news is an interesting appropriation of the term that can be credited to Donald Trump. In a 2018 tweet, Trump said: '91% of the network news about me is Negative (fake)'.[6] This idea of 'fake news' as used by the former US President does not fit neatly into any of the first six categories. The content of the statement is rather revealing about this particular use of the term. Instead of referring to the veracity of information, in this context it refers to the relationship between the information and its subject. 'Fake' here means undesirable. Any news that does not shine a positive light on its subject is dismissed as 'fake news' (the meaning conflates unfavourable and untrue).

Donald Trump's lawyer Rudy Giuliani explained this approach with the phrase 'Truth isn't truth' – meaning: this is the world as I'd like to see it, irrespective of facts. It's ultimately an issue of clearly differentiating facts from opinions.[7] Both facts and opinions can be genuine and legitimate, but must be clearly separated. Good news sources do this by clearly separating news from editorial. The line on social media is often more blurred, so the responsibility falls upon the reader to distinguish between facts, fabrication and opinion.

The challenge for business

Good, successful businesses operate on accurate information. Any business needs to understand its people and performance. Information about the market and competitors is essential for operating successfully. Knowledge about laws and regulations is necessary to maintain and run a business. Accurate information about customers and clients is vital for a company to provide goods or services.

Effective decision-making in business relies on using good information. Economic and labour market forecasts, consumer demand, market research and regulatory environments will all affect business performance. The decisions made by leaders of teams, departments and companies will rely on the most accurate information and the best available projections.

Let's use the example of a company looking for a new location to build a call centre in the UK. The company needs a relatively large, mobile workforce who can be trained relatively quickly and develop further skills while working.

There are two potential sources of information about the number of workers available in the chosen location. Firstly, there is a former factory owner turned local politician who campaigned on reducing unemployment. This politician runs a social media account that posts publicity photos in factories, alongside photos of empty job centres. The running theme from their social media is that unemployment has been drastically reduced in the area. Secondly, government numbers from the Office of National Statistics (ONS) show relatively high unemployment in the area, which suggests there are many people looking for work.

Let's assume that both are relatively accurate in their portrayal. The first shows genuine photos of people working and empty job centres. The second represents accurate numbers for the overall proportion of people who are unemployed in the area. Who is to be believed? Which is the best source of information for a business?

There isn't necessarily a clear-cut answer here. Large, national representative research conducted by a reliable organization with rigorous research methods like the ONS tends to be the most consistently reliable. As a general rule, numbers from the ONS would be much more reliable for making an initial assessment.

But effective business intelligence should consider both sources of information and thoughtfully weigh the credibility of each. Social media may be a good start in reaching out to people in the area for more information and contacts. Initial research may lead to a visit to that area.

During the visit you might chat to taxi drivers about how business is in the area, check out the local shops and job centres, or talk to the chambers of commerce or a leading business and industry association. Social media is a great way of assessing opinions, but it is supplementary to, not a replacement for, first-hand research.

Evaluating information

Susan Nolan writes for the American Psychological Association about evaluating fake news.[8] One simple and effective method for evaluating the veracity of information is a framework with a pleasing acronym: the CRAAP test.[9]

This uses five categories to evaluate information and its source. Each category comes with some questions the reader should consider about the source to assess its trustworthiness:

1 **Currency**: the timeliness of the information. Is it recent, and has it been updated? Is there more recent information available, or will older sources work as well?
2 **Relevance**: how important the information is for you. Is it sufficiently simple or advanced for your requirements? Have you looked at other sources to see if it is relevant to you? Would you be comfortable relying on this source of information?
3 **Authority**: the source of the information. Is it reliable? Can you tell who published the information? Is it from a real person or organization? Is there contact information, or is it anonymous?

4 **Accuracy:** the reliability of the information. Is it supported by good evidence? Any evidence? Can the information be verified using another reliable source? Does the language seem unbiased and free from errors?

5 **Purpose:** the reason for the information existing. What is the purpose of the information? Does it intend to argue, teach, sell, entertain, persuade or call to action? Is the purpose clear? Is it fact, opinion, advertising or propaganda?

Strong, healthy businesses run on facts, good research and credible information. Business decisions need to be made based on evidence. Businesses should be particularly careful about evaluating information that is to be used in decision-making or planning. We talk about the particulars of using social media in business and advertising in detail in Myth 27.

Conclusion

Misinformation, parody and satire exist, as they always have, in different mediums and formats. But social media is not full of fake news; it is highly dependent on who you follow and what content you interact with. It's essential to use trusted sources, critical thinking and to be a cautious consumer of media, irrespective of the platform.

Notes

1   Mansky, J (2018) The age-old problem of 'Fake News', *Smithsonian Magazine*, www.smithsonianmag.com/history/age-old-problem-fake-news-180968945 (archived at https://perma.cc/EZL6-3LRY)

2 Lazer, D M et al (2018) The science of fake news, *Science*, **359** (6380), pp 1094–96

3 Tandoc, E C, Lim, Z W and Ling, R (2018) Defining 'Fake News': A typology of scholarly definitions, *Digital Journalism*, **6** (2), pp 137–53

4 MacRae, I (2021) *Dark Social: Understanding the darker side of work, personality and social media*, Bloomsbury, London

5 Farsetta, D (2006) Fake TV news: Widespread and undisclosed, *PR Watch*, www.prwatch.org/fakenews/execsummary (archived at https://perma.cc/8PPD-QPF8)

6 Retrieved from https://twitter.com/realDonaldTrump/status/994179864436596736 (archived at https://perma.cc/7FJ5-ZVUJ)

7 BBC (2018) Trump lawyer Rudy Giuliani: Truth isn't truth: www.bbc.co.uk/news/world-us-canada-45241838 (archived at https://perma.cc/3TZN-JUXJ)

8 Nolan, S (2017) Critical thinking and information fluency: Fake news in the classroom, *APA*, www.apa.org/ed/precollege/ptn/2017/05/fake-news (archived at https://perma.cc/SUK7-GEVV)

9 Blakeslee, S (2004) The CRAAP test, *LOEX Quarterly*, **31** (3), pp 6–7

MYTH 24

Social media is the best source of information

One of the challenges of having such vast quantities of information easily available is that more choice does not always lead to better decision-making.

Whatever is happening, wherever it is in the world, if someone has seen it happen they probably want to talk about it. We are social animals who share information. In the information era, social media is the default for many in sharing, spreading or looking for information.

Social media is a hotspot for raw, unfiltered and immediate information. That's not the only type of information, and it's not always easy to identify which information is earnest or honest – but it is possible.

There is, of course, fake news, false information and propaganda all over social media (as we discuss in detail in Myth 23). This means that finding accurate information on social media can be a bit of a filtering exercise. But as we discuss in Myth 25, it is possible to shape your own social media environment to be dominated by trustworthy and reliable sources of information.

Finding trusted sources

The main point of this myth is that social media can be an excellent source of information – when the source is credible.

Research from Gallup and UNICEF in 2021 found that most social media users are sceptical about the information they see on social media. Only 12 per cent of people over 40 and 17 per cent of people aged 15 to 24 said they had a lot of trust in social media sites to provide accurate information.[1]

The source of information changes the level of trust in the information, although people may not have a lot of trust in the platform *in general,* and when people are polled about trusting various platforms online, the responses tend to indicate relatively low levels of trust. Yet research finds trust in specific people and sources is much higher. When information is shared by someone that a person trusts, they are far more likely to like, share and discuss that news story. But people struggle to differentiate between trustworthy news sources and fictional ones; they place a lot more trust in the person sharing the story than the source of the story. [2]

Social media often has two points of reference for trust, because much of the information is originally posted by one source, then shared by someone else. Both these sources influence how people view the information:

- **Trust in the person who shared the article.** When people see information from a trusted source, they are more likely to believe the article 'got the facts right'. People are also far more likely to share the article or recommend it to friends when it comes from a trusted source.
- **Trust in the original source.** In a 2017 study,[3] two groups of people were shown an article and told that it came from either a made-up source or the Associated Press. Unsurprisingly, most were more likely to believe that the article was accurate when they believed that it was by the Associated Press. However, those who reported not trusting mainstream news sources were far more likely to believe the article when they thought it came from a publication they hadn't heard of.

The message is both clear and unsurprising: people are influenced by those they trust. This doesn't entirely answer the question of whether social media as a whole is a good source of information. It does show that both the source and the person sharing information influence people's assessment of the trustworthiness of information.

One major concern is when people 'trust' unreliable sources. Of course, there are some prominent people and organizations that are less than reliable and honest. Added to this, there are a staggering number of fake accounts on social media. Facebook alone deleted 3 billion fake accounts between October 2018 and March 2019[4] and then another 4.5 billion accounts in 2020.[5]

A balanced diet of information

The internet has made information easy, fast and cheap to access for everyone, and it has become increasingly widely used by all types of users, from casual searchers to academics. But one of the challenges of having such vast quantities of information easily available is that more choice does not always lead to better decision-making.

When looking for information, people tend to look for the most accessible information source, even if it is not the most accurate. When people have questions about their health, for example, where do most people go first? Their GP? Friends? Family? No, from pregnancy to kidney problems, most people's first source of information is the internet, and recent years have accelerated that trend. When people are more anxious they are more likely to search for medical information online. And when people are more anxious, they tend to be less critical about evaluating the source of the information.[6]

Study after study has shown that convenience is the most important factor in choosing information sources. However, when you're making business decisions, accuracy needs to be prioritized over convenience. Better-quality information will lead to better decision-making. Myth 23 provides a framework for evaluating information.

It may also be useful to judge sources based on the amount of time they take to be published. Generally, those with a longer publication timescale go through a more rigorous and discerning editorial process. Table 24.1 shows how different information sources have greatly different publication timescales. Information can be posted on

TABLE 24.1 Sources based on publication timescale

Publication timescale	Sources	Content	Intended audience	Written by
Seconds	Social media, blogs, radio, TV	News reporting, quick summary information and commentary	General public or specific interest groups	Anyone
Days	Newspapers, TV, radio	News and commentary	General public	Journalists, subject matter experts
Weeks	Popular magazines	Popular topics for general or specialist audiences	General public	Journalists, subject matter experts
Months	Scholarly journals	Research results and scientific analysis	Academics, specialists, students	Academics, specialists in the field
1+ years	Books	In-depth coverage of a specific topic	General audience, audience with interest in specific topic	Academics, specialists, subject matter experts
5+ years	Reference sources, textbooks	Big-picture, factual information which may include all of the above sources	General audience, audience with interest in specific topic	Specialists, subject matter experts

Source: Adapted from UCF Libraries, The Information Cycle

social media within seconds, while lengthy and well-researched works can take months or even years to be published.

A well-researched publication that has gone through a rigorous editorial process by a reliable and trustworthy publisher can be regarded as a good information source. But there may be overlap between the different sources. This book cites a range of sources, from social media and magazines to scientific journals, books and textbooks. To take another example, the quotes at the beginning of each myth may be regarded as a 'snapshot' of the information within. However, the full text provides much more detail and context.

Another way to evaluate a source is to look at how long it has been available. Books, for example, tend to get lengthier and more in-depth critiques than fleeting social media posts. This can make it easier to evaluate the quality of a source based on the opinions of reputable third parties, as well as the reputation of the author and publisher.

Conclusion

Social media is not always the best source of accurate information. News from your social feeds can form part of a balanced diet of information consumption, but don't make it your only source. This is particularly important in business when decision-making can affect huge numbers of staff, customers or profitability.

Notes

1 Young people rely on social media, but don't trust it: https://news.
   gallup.com/opinion/gallup/357446/young-people-rely-social-media-don-
   trust.aspx (archived at https://perma.cc/C3NQ-YDAM)

2 Sterrett, D et al (2019) Who shared it?: Deciding what news to trust on
   social media: *Digital Journalism*, 7 (6), pp 783–801 DOI 10.1080/
   21670811.2019.1623702 (archived at https://perma.cc/2RJU-JZ32)

3 'Who shared it?': How Americans decide what news to trust on social
   media: www.americanpressinstitute.org/publications/reports/survey-
   research/trust-social-media (archived at https://perma.cc/8FEG-AVZH)

4 Facebook: Another three billion fake profiles culled: www.bbc.co.uk/
   news/technology-48380504 (archived at https://perma.cc/7NYE-YE32)

5 Why can't the social networks stop fake accounts? https://www.nytimes.
   com/2020/12/08/technology/why-cant-the-social-networks-stop-fake-
   accounts.html (archived at https://perma.cc/MGJ2-M4AN)

6 Freiling, I, Krause, N M, Scheufele, D A and Brossard, D (2021)
   Believing and sharing misinformation, fact checks, and accurate
   information on social media: The role of anxiety during COVID-19,
   New Media & Society: https://doi.org/10.1177/14614448211011451
   (archived at https://perma.cc/ZW9U-HU59)

MYTH 25

Social media intensifies information bubbles

The idea that certain individuals or groups are only exposed to self-selected content is nothing new, and certainly not an invention of social media.

Everything is personalized online. The early days of the internet were all about accessing information, but now all online activity involves sharing your own personal information – whether you are aware of it or not. That allows everyone to receive their own, tailored, digital experience. Yet this happens subtly, and can influence people in ways that may not be immediately apparent.

The question is whether, and to what degree, people are exposed to information and opinion from outside their own interest groups. Most people are aware that their online experience has some degree of personalization, but how much awareness do most people have about what *other people's* digital experiences are like? A group of people who are only exposed to a very narrow view of information and opinion are said to exist in a 'filter bubble'.

There is a tendency for bubbles of information and opinion to form online, and particularly on social media, as there is in the real world. In this myth we'll look at issues concerning bubbles, including how isolating they really are, and the role of social media. How do companies interact with different information bubbles, or groupings of people, online? Is this something that businesses need to take special measures to manage, or is it just a natural phenomenon that emerges from regular social interaction? Do businesses, departments and teams end up in their own bubbles?

To clarify, throughout the rest of the myth we will use the term 'filter bubbles' to describe social groups or environments where only specific types of information or opinion exist, while much is filtered out.

Do filter bubbles exist?

There has been a good deal of scientific research investigating the cause and effects of filter bubbles, going back at least 70 years. The idea that certain individuals or groups are only exposed to self-selected content is nothing new, and certainly not an invention of social media.

Although filter bubbles exist, the research would indicate their effects are modest, at best, for the majority of people.[1] People do tend to look for information they agree with, and social media algorithms show people content similar to previous content they have seen. However, popularity seems to be a much stronger influence than ideology. 'Trending topics' and information that is widely shared cuts through most ideological filter bubbles. On social media, it is actually much harder to avoid all dissenting points of view.

A study by Flaxman and colleagues in 2016 started by analysing the online behaviour of 1.2 million Americans. It then narrowed down the sample group to 50,000 people who met all the study criteria (including being regular online news consumers). Their research showed that although people tend to have moderate preferences towards sources that aligned with their political beliefs, most users accessed sources across the political divide. Both Republicans and Democrats accessed stories from a range of sources. There was a small amount of bias, but the effect was modest. The large majority of those interested in political news did not appear to exist in a bubble.[2]

There are limitations to the research, partly because the focus was on mainstream news sources, and partly because participants were, by definition, part of a group that were happy to share their data. However, the general conclusion is that most people in their study were not too polarized, and not living entirely in a bubble.

The other implication, though, is that the smaller segments with more extreme views are more likely to exist in a bubble, and their bubbles are likely to be less porous.

How filter bubbles are created

It is not new for people to seek out content, information and opinions that are like beliefs they already hold. Psychologists call this 'confirmation bias'. The phenomenon was originally described by psychologists in the 1960s to explain a natural tendency in human behaviour that has existed throughout history.

Filter bubbles and bias are not new to politics, either. The earliest research on political confirmation bias and filter bubbles goes back to research conducted during the 1940 US presidential election. Democrats were more likely to be exposed to Democratic campaigning, and Republicans were more likely to be exposed to Republican campaigning.[3] Not very surprising, but perhaps comforting to know that filter bubbles are not unique to the online environment.

There are similar examples from other countries where those on the left tend to read left-leaning publications, while those on the right side of the political spectrum read right-leaning publications. Catholics read Catholic publications while Protestants read Protestant publications. Research from the Netherlands by Borgesius and colleagues found that this trend goes back through the 20th century.[4]

So, confirmation bias is not a phenomenon that has emerged out of the internet and social media. Social media, however, does have the potential to make seeking information congruent with your own worldview very quick and easy. So, the question is worth asking: is social media exacerbating these natural tendencies?

There are two ways that the online environment is a bit different to everyday life. First, a staggeringly wide range of news and opinions is quickly and easily available – so it is much easier for people to create their own online bubbles. Second, search engines and social media sites do filter information based on what they think their users might already want to see.

Borgesius and colleagues describe these two different ways bubbles can be created:

1 **Self-selecting personalization** is when people choose content that aligns with their worldview. This is classic confirmation bias. For example, people with a strong political ideology are likely to read publications that tell them what they want to hear (read how a fake news website capitalized on this in Myth 23). Or conspiracy theorists may be drawn in deeper to deeply strange belief systems by seeking out information. For example, if you believe the Earth is flat and you search for content that supports that belief online, you will find some.

2 **Pre-selected personalization** is when there are filters that go on in the background of search engines, websites and social media. The algorithms dictate what a person sees – typically based on what they have looked at before, their demographics, previous social media activity or any other data they have left from their footprints online. This happens without the user consenting, or necessarily even knowing that it's happening.

These two types of personalized filter bubbles can feed into each other as well. For example, if you have been searching about 'Flat Earth' theories, your social media accounts will be more likely to show you related pages and adverts. YouTube will start recommending conspiracy theory videos, and Amazon will happily advertise the tinfoil you might need to make your own hat.

If filter bubbles are a natural social phenomenon that could be amplified by social media online, what are the implications for business?

The business implications

Let's look at how filter bubbles can have an impact in a workplace or organization. Within a company, people pre-select their own filter bubbles by choosing to interact with colleagues who work in the same team or department, or people they need to interact with regularly to get their job done. A company's internal social media could also create pre-selected filter bubbles by prioritizing information from certain people within the company that have similar roles and responsibilities.

On the surface, people are likely to have a level of both self-selecting personalization and pre-selected personalization in their social networks by the nature of where they work. Take, for example, LinkedIn. People are more likely to connect with those in similar positions, at the same employer or in a similar sector. Because of that, people are likely to cultivate connections with those who have a similar background and experience to them, and consequently will tend to be exposed to similar content. It is likely that people who work for an oil and gas company, for example, will see very different content than people who work for an environmental charity. This, too, should not be surprising. It is an amplification of what happens naturally in the workplace.

Issues to consider

There are a range of issues, opportunities and risks associated with filter bubbles in social media. These are not necessarily positive or negative, but form a useful framework for discussing the business implications:

- **Polarization.** One of the issues with social media bubbles is that they have the potential to drive people with different opinions further apart and reduce levels of agreement or understanding between groups. For businesses this poses an obvious opportunity, along with a serious risk. It makes it relatively easy to target a particular group and play upon the attitudes within that group. For example, one political group may have a series of jokes, imagery and memes they use in a humorous context. It may be tempting to use those jokes in a marketing campaign to appear to a certain group. The risk of polarization for businesses is that attempts to appeal to one group could alienate other groups.
- **New gatekeepers and influencers.** The traditional gatekeepers of information and opinion were people like press barons, public censors or state regulators. Now content providers such as app stores, social media websites and search engines are major gatekeepers and influencers.

These are the organizations which provide pre-selected personalization. In the case of social media platforms, who as major advertising organizations provide hyper-targeting and pre-selected personalization – these new gatekeepers are often far more powerful than the traditional news barons. Popular companies and users on these platforms have also become major influencers.

- **Concerns about autonomy.** Filter bubbles have the potential to either increase or diminish personal autonomy and independence. Self-selected personalization can increase the breadth of information people have access to. Conversely, some would argue pre-selected personalization reduces personal autonomy when people's options online are limited to a very specific range that has been chosen for them, instead of opening up access.
- **Lack of transparency.** An ongoing concern about pre-selection filter bubbles is that many online giants do not make their algorithms public, and people do not know exactly how they are being influenced. Organizations would be advised to be as transparent as possible about the ways they use and interact with social media. This is discussed in much more detail in Myths 21 and 23.
- **Social sorting.** Another concern raised about social media is the risks associated with sorting people into different categories. This may create problems, but it is certainly not uncommon or new. In business it's known as market segmentation. The capacity to easily identify and target communications to specific groups or individuals is fantastically useful for businesses. There are many legitimate and ethical ways to do this, but problems arise when the practices are discriminatory or disadvantage certain

groups (for example, targeting job advertisements at a particular demographic group). Recent research has found social media algorithms can introduce significant racial bias into targeted marketing, even when that is not the advertiser's intention.[5] This, like many of the issues raised, is extremely important to consider, because making mistakes (even out of ignorance rather than malice) can create serious ethical, legal and business problems.

Conclusion

This is not a myth – social media does have the capacity to intensify information bubbles. Businesses need to be aware that filter bubbles exist to varying degrees. There are advantages, because any business strategy relies on a common vision for the organization and the people who work there. Internal use of social media and an online presence can enhance this. Bubbles are also, essentially, market segments, so this makes it easy to target potential customers, clients or employees online. But there are also disadvantages. Companies need to guard against becoming too insular and falling into bubbles where they are disconnected from outside viewpoints. This will rarely lead to good decision-making or policy.

Notes

1 Möller, J (2021) Filter bubbles and digital echo chambers. In H Tumber and S Waisbord (eds) *The Routledge Companion to Media Disinformation and Populism*, Routledge, London

2   Flaxman, S, Goel, S and Rao, J M (2016) Filter bubbles, echo chambers, and online news consumption, *Public Opinion Quarterly*, 80 (**S1**), pp 298–320

3   Lazarsfeld, P F, Berelson, B and Gaudet, H (1944) *The People's Choice: How the voter makes up his mind in a presidential campaign*, Columbia University Press, New York

4   Borgesius, F J Z et al (2016) Should we worry about filter bubbles? *Internet Policy Review*, 5 (1)

5   Facebook's ad algorithm discriminates even when it's not told to, study finds: http://nymag.com/intelligencer/2019/04/facebooks-ad-algorithm-is-a-fully-functional-racism-machine.html (archived at https://perma.cc/ERB9-TT68)

MYTH 26

Social media is not strategic

*Right message, right person, right time. If you're in the
restaurant business, posting photos of your food may
be a key component of your social media strategy.*

The advantage (and the disadvantage) of social media is
that the content is what you choose to make it. Some
people will tell you that social media activity is a great way
to connect with people; others will say social media is full
of conflict and vitriol. Both may be right, and the reason is
that when it comes to social media, you engineer your own
social circle, discussion topics, advertising environment
and discourse.

For businesses, participating in social media is not about
engaging with every person, on every level, in every location about all topics. A strategic approach, aligned with
organizational purpose and focus, goes a very long way.

Components of your social media strategy

The following aspects should be considered when building out your social media strategy:

1 Start with the end in mind:
   – Who are we as a brand and an organization?
   – What are our purpose and values?
   – What mission are we on?
   – How does this align with our brand story and cascade through our content?
   – How does it cascade through our 'always on' social media brand channels?

2 Situation analysis. Research and analyse the following to establish where you are and where you want to get to:
   – Where do we sit in our market?
   – Where do we sit with our customers/audiences/competitors?
   – What's the opportunity?
   – A simple SWOT analysis can help you see where you are, the opportunities you seek and challenges that you may need to overcome.

3 Objectives and goals. Your social media activity should align with wider organizational objectives. Understanding the bigger picture enables you to focus on what matters. Ask yourself:
   – What do we want to achieve via our social media activity?
   – What does success look like?
   – How can social media drive ROI?

4 Channels:
   –   Which social channels are going to be part of our mix?
   –   Which channels do we currently have, and which are performing?
   –   Where is our audience?
   –   Are we simply filling the feeds or are we focused on being where our audience is?
   –   How does each channel operate?
   –   Which channels fit with our objectives?
   –   How can we optimize each channel?

5 Tactics:
   –   What's our plan of action?
   –   Which channels do we need and why?
   –   What's our supportive content strategy? Do we have our voice and tone sorted? Are we going to create, reuse, curate and repurpose media content?
   –   Who is relevant to our brand/organization?
   –   Which partners or influencers can we collaborate with?
   –   Consider budgets and POEM – paid, owned and earned media. How are we splitting out our activity across paid and organic – is it balanced and are we ensuring that community management is still part of our paid activity?
   –   Are we learning from doing and utilizing data-driven insights?
   –   Are we listening – and learning from listening? Are we acting on social listening insights?

6 Measurement and KPIs. Ensure that you are using the social signals to learn about what's progressing well, or not, while keeping an eye on the bigger picture business signals. Your strategy needs to be optimized to deliver on those. Ask yourself the following:
- Are we measuring what really matters?
- Is our measurement informed by our 'bigger picture' objectives?
- Are we only measuring social signals (likes, followers, engagement) or are we also focused on business signals (leads, brand sentiment, partnerships, sales)?

Focus on the right audience

As demonstrated in the case study below, social media is most effective when the channels are planned in line with your strategic endeavours. It gives a clear message and purpose. Liken it to someone showing up to give a press conference completely unprepared. What they end up saying could be surprising, off-message and confusing to their audience and the presenter. However, having clear objectives enables you to tailor the content, shape the messaging and align with the appropriate channels.

This is where social media for personal use sharply diverges from business use. Many people choose to have individual social media accounts to share, discuss and post about whatever they want. Businesses would be unwise to take the same approach with their social media 'brand'-focused accounts. This doesn't mean that business-related social media activity cannot be spontaneous, informal, fun, personal or even a bit unpredictable. But for businesses, their social media activity should fit within a framework of what the company does, who they are, and what they want to communicate in a contextual way, aligning with those with whom they are communicating.

Finding the right channels

Once you know who your customer is (or have defined the characteristics your customers have) you get a better sense of who they are and why they might be interested in your business. It then becomes more straightforward to understand which social channels they are using, and what might appeal to them on those channels.

It's all about getting the right message on the right channels to the right audiences in a way that meets your audiences where they are at. You want to draw them into your sphere of influence and get them to know you, like you and trust you. Ultimately, you want to maximize share of mind and have people do business with you, refer you, or become more loyal to you.

CASE STUDY Tonkotsu

To get some additional insight into specific examples of best practice and professional insight on social media, we spoke to Ashleigh Muir, Brand Manager at Tonkotsu.

Tonkotsu is a ramen restaurant with locations in Birmingham and London. It started up in London in 2012, enjoyed great success and grew quickly to 10 locations. In 2019, they secured additional investment funding to open further locations.[1]

Their key content – food – works very well in a visual medium. Food reviewers love a sensual description, so it's best to use their words: 'And then the deep, luscious Tonkotsu ramen arrived filled with silky noodles, slices of soft pork belly, half a seasoned soft-boiled egg and with a slick of black garlic oil across the top.'[2] But times are moving on, and getting good photos of great-looking food online can be even more effective than a delectable review in *The Times* or the *Guardian*.

Interview

Ashleigh Muir, Tonkotsu's brand manager, estimates that about 40 per cent of Tonkotsu's new customers discover them first on social media. She said it can be challenging to estimate exactly how many people visit the restaurant as a direct result of discovering them on social channels. But on channels like Instagram, they get a very good sense of the interest online, and analytics tools are useful for understanding how many people engage with their posts and share them with others. And, of course, when the food looks great people want to come in and share photos of their meals.

Muir describes Tonkotsu's overall approach to their social media presence as 'informative, but fairly relaxed'. They use it to share images of the restaurant, the food and people enjoying themselves. A combination of more relaxed and fun photos, and great food at the physical locations, helps the food to sell itself. 'We tend to use it as a tool to share great imagery of our fantastic food, and for connecting with our followers in a fun way, instead of heavily advertising with lots of calls to action and "click this and do that"-type advertising,' Muir says.

Their social media has always been handled internally. It was initially managed by the founders, but Muir took over the accounts once she joined as brand manager. She has sole responsibility for the company's social media activity, saying she may decide to share this with other employees in future, but plans to always keep it internal.

She describes how their social media activity has changed both with the growth of the company and the rise of social media. 'We've always used social media, but we rely on it a lot more these days than we did back in 2012. For us, social media is the quickest and most efficient way to share news and information with our followers and potential new customers.'

Muir thinks video-based channels are likely to become even more influential. 'Video seems to be the next big thing, with apps like TikTok and Lasso becoming very popular,' she says. 'Businesses need to understand these trends, and be open to using new platforms, switching and sometimes leaving old platforms behind. Using the same platforms as your target customer is always important to stay relevant, so there may be a platform we pick up or leave behind in future.'

It also leads nicely into the advice Muir has for new businesses starting out on social media: 'Don't fall into the trap of paying people to get you new followers.' She advises a slower, more deliberate and strategic approach. Get more people interested in your business as it grows, have a great product, and post about it on social. 'Growing your following and engagement is best done organically, by posting great imagery with engaging captions. It's not worth getting your account shut down over! Slow and steady wins the race.'

When I asked her what she likes to see from their customers on social media, Muir said, 'We love it when customers share snaps of their food, or of them enjoying their time in our restaurants. We quite often repost them and share them with our own followers. We also welcome any feedback (positive or negative) through any of our social channels. We want to be easily contactable by whatever way is best for our customers.'

Strategy summary

Key points summarizing Tonkotsu's social media strategy:

- accounts are internally managed;
- a focus on visually oriented posts (ideal for Instagram), showing visually appealing products;
- a blend of organic and some activated paid social advertising;
- a fun, informal style;
- a post frequency of about five times per week;
- a focus on encouraging user-generated content and co-creation of content.

Conclusion

It's vital to align social media activity with strategic objectives. Understand where your audiences are, what matters to them, the problems you're solving and the tactics you're applying to engage them. Right message, right person, right time. If you're in the restaurant business, posting photos of your food may be a key component of your social media strategy.

Measure your activity in a way that aligns with strategic goals. 'Social signals' such as likes, comments and engagement are useful for understanding how your content is landing and if you're attracting the right audiences; they don't necessarily drive tangible business results. Get clear on how social media can support those bottom-line outcomes and set meaningful KPIs and metrics that matter, whether that's building awareness, new audiences, entering new territories, developing new partnerships or lead generation.

Notes

1 Ramen chain Tonkotsu eyes expansion with YFM backing: www.cityam.com/ramen-chain-tonkotsu-eyes-expansion-with-yfm-backing (archived at https://perma.cc/B2QK-MHPY)
2 Restaurant review: Tonkotsu, London: www.theguardian.com/lifeandstyle/2012/nov/25/tonkotsu-restaurant-review-jay-rayner (archived at https://perma.cc/AU8V-3JQ9)

MYTH 27

Social media is purely for broadcasting

What better way is there of engaging with people than by letting them know you are listening and that their views, issues, gripes and insights matter?

When it comes to social media, this myth is still taken literally by far too many people, brands and organizations.

Take a look at random business accounts on Twitter, LinkedIn or Facebook – and you'll often see a stream of promotional, one-way broadcast posts. Consistent, yes! Yet often with zero or very low engagement.

Far from being socially engaged with audiences, it's very clear that the whole purpose of many accounts is purely to broadcast. In fact, the focus on broadcasting overrides any opportunity for genuine engagement – so much so that comments, shares, retweets or other signals of engagement are often totally ignored. The two-way conversational aspect of 'being social' just isn't part of the remit.

The focus is purely one-way. And that doesn't bode well if markets are conversations!

The 80/20 ratio

We like the analogy: two eyes, two ears, and just the one mouth. This approach to broadcasting equates to a ratio of approximately 80 per cent listening and 20 per cent broadcasting. Eighty per cent of the time you should be tuned in, responding, elaborating, extending, educating and entertaining, and 20 per cent of the time you are directly promoting.

Yet theory clearly doesn't drive real-world action. A study by Sprout Social found that brands share 23 promotional messages for every message they respond to.[1] If we extrapolate that to total social media activity, the balance ratio equates to 4 per cent of activity focused on responding, and 96 per cent on promotion. A far cry from the theoretical 80/20 balance.

It's clear to see where this myopia emerges from: one-way broadcasting has been used since advertising took off in the 1930s. TV advertising, press advertising, trade-press advertorials, magazine editorials, billboard advertising, direct mail and even radio all focus on pushing messages to audiences. They do this regardless of whether there's desire from the audience to engage.

When social channels emerged, they were simply seen as new channels to market largely adopted by marketing departments and managed as part of the marketing channel mix to extend the broadcast messaging of campaigns. For some organizations, this marketing-centric 'push' focus is still very much the case.

However, social media channels differ considerably from traditional linear channels. Social media enables networked conversations. A range of one-to-one, one-to-many and many-to-many conversations are facilitated, with peers, colleagues, friends, strangers, influencers, brands, organizations, leaders, thought leaders, authors, product developers and even world leaders – a complex hive of connected conversations.

Beyond broadcasting

Using social channels purely to push promotional messages is therefore short-sighted and ignores the numerous opportunities that social media enables. Over the past decade, it's become apparent that social media channels offer organizations and brands the opportunity to tune into audiences – the largest focus group available. Crimson Hexagon's survey of digital marketing professionals revealed that nearly three-quarters (72 per cent) believed monitoring public sentiment via social media is just as good, if not better, than using traditional focus groups.[2] Meltwater's research agrees: 'When you've got two billion active Facebook users a month ready and waiting to give you their opinion, the focus group doesn't stand a chance.'[3]

Social networks provide scope for customer insight which looking back just 15–20 years, would have been met with jaw-dropping awe. Tuning in and listening via social media in real time presents significant opportunity for organizations. However, when there's too much emphasis on pushing out promotional messages, these chances to engage with customers are lost.

Listening to customers and developing two-way conversations enables organizations to develop their operations in the following areas.

Customer service

It's commonplace for brands and organizations to manage customer queries and complaints via social media channels. This ranges from supermarkets to public transport services, police services, hospital services, doctors and schools, and large corporations through to microbusinesses.

The Sprout Social report mentioned earlier identifies that when it comes to customer service, around a third of people prefer to reach out to organizations via social media rather than calling them, visiting their website or using live chat. That same report also highlights the somewhat disturbing findings that 89 per cent of such messages to organizations are totally ignored!

Rather than serving their audiences on social media, the reality is that far too many organizations are failing to truly tune in, listen and respond. As Scott Stratten and Alison Kramer succinctly put it in their book *UnMarketing*: 'It's like turning up to a networking event wearing earplugs.'[4]

Brand and relationship building

Failure to respond to customer queries doesn't just ignore the need to serve the customer and develop positive brand value – it also misses the opportunity to build and strengthen relationships with customers. How impressed would you be by a brand or organization if you bothered to share your opinion with them, or raised a question, and received zero response?

What better way is there of engaging with people than by letting them know you are listening and that their views, issues, gripes and insights matter? We all want, and increasingly expect, to be heard. It's not just about mutual respect, however; it's also good for business.

Customer service statistics gathered by Helpscout bring to light the impact of positive and negative brand experiences.[5] On the negative side:

- 88 per cent of consumers aren't as likely to buy from companies who don't answer their complaints;
- it takes 12 good experiences to make up for one bad experience;
- unhappy customers will tell between 9 and 15 people about a bad experience;
- 30 per cent of customers who are shunned by brands on social media are more likely to switch to a competitor.

On the positive side:

- customers who feel engaged by companies on social media will spend up to 40 per cent more with them than other customers;
- 81 per cent are more likely to buy from a business again after a good service experience.

You'd think these statistics alone (and there are many others) would ensure social monitoring and listening to audiences was considered a priority.

Listening is gold

According to Domo's infographic 'Data Never Sleeps', every minute of every day:

- Snapchat users send 2 million snapchats
- Twitter users post 575,000 tweets
- Instagram users share 65,000 photos
- Facebook Live receives 44 million views
- YouTube users stream 694,000 hours
- TikTok users watch 167 million videos[6]

The data is beyond big and the volume of real-time conversation is staggering, providing significant amounts of insight and sentiment for research teams, agencies and organizations to analyse and draw valuable business intelligence from.

The opportunity for listening, whether at a sophisticated or basic level, is readily available. As discussed in Myth 8, sophisticated enterprise solutions are available to help organizations uncover sentiment and carry out competitor analysis.

Listening can assist with several practical insights:

- **Customer sentiment** – how your customers are feeling, what they're talking about, how, where and when they engage.
- **Corporate messaging** – the ability to listen and respond to sentiment appropriately, whether that's defending your brand's reputation or position, educating audiences with thought leadership, or engaging audiences on a topic around brand values.

- **Competitor sentiment** – watching what your competitors are doing, the sentiment of their audiences (useful for opportunity spotting), as well as measuring your share of voice against competitors. In an interview one of the authors conducted with John Legere, former CEO of T-Mobile US, he described how tuning into competitors and the feedback from their audiences helps him to drive innovation around new product development.[7]
- **Brand awareness and share of voice** – gaining a general understanding of your positioning in the marketplace.
- **Brand sentiment** – finding out how people feel about your brand.
- **Product development** – people may be having conversations about how your product or service performs. Innovation and development ideas can be gleaned directly from those actively using the product. Use your customers to learn how you can improve the user experience – who better to give you insights than those already using and talking about your products?
- **Influencer relationship development** – listening enables you to spot who the influential people are in your networks – your advocates helping to amplify your brand, products and awareness generally. Identifying such influencers, thanking them, and developing relationships with them, can provide a smart way to continuously optimize reach and influence in an authentic way.

While most listening on social media focuses on brand mentions – those instances where users have tagged a brand or an organization – it's also worth tracking misspelled or generic (untagged) mentions of your brand or organization name too.

Social listening within the organization

Whether adopting enterprise social networking systems or creating their own proprietary social networks, an increasing number of organizations are using social technologies as internal communication platforms (which we explored more closely in Myth 13). Here, the same listening principles apply.

As with consumers, if an organization simply considers social networking as a platform for corporate communications, broadcasting and pushing out promotional messages in a linear way to internal audiences, then again, this misses the point of connected, social, networked conversations. You may fail to optimize collaboration between employees across departments, or miss the opportunity to hear from team members who prefer not to share ideas in an open forum.

Companies should ensure that there are processes and systems in place to listen to employees and sentiment. It's equally important to respond in a timely and productive way to encourage continuous authentic engagement, relationship development and overall success. Findings from Novartis suggest a 12 per cent increase in employee satisfaction after implementing social media to engage and connect with staff.[8]

Social channels are highly practical for reaching new audiences, brand building and sharing messages – but let's not forget that they are networks. They are not one-way broadcast channels; they facilitate connected conversations.

Conclusion

Social media is not all about broadcasting. Listening should never be underestimated. It's a key sense that aids human survival, which is equally relevant for business survival. Focused listening helps inform what you broadcast, so that your communications and content are more useful and purposeful and your audiences are compelled to engage.

Social media technologies give you the opportunity to tune in to your customers, to broaden your audience and reach those you may not ordinarily have the chance to connect with; to build and strengthen relationships and harness knowledge and insights.

Very simply, don't make social media all about you – but, instead, all about them.

Notes

1 The Sprout Social Index, Edition VI: Shunning your customers on social? https://sproutsocial.com/insights/data/q2-2016/ (archived at https://perma.cc/7WMA-Z52N)

2 72% of professionals see social media as a more reliable source of public sentiment than traditional focus groups: www.thedrum.com/news/2013/10/15/72-professionals-see-social-media-more-reliable-source-public-sentiment-traditional (archived at https://perma.cc/J9KY-74ZQ)

3 Focus groups are dead, thanks to social media: https://mumbrella.com.au/social-media-was-the-final-nail-in-the-focus-groups-coffin-462210 (archived at https://perma.cc/5AZY-78CN)

4 Stratten, S and Kramer, A (2012) *UnMarketing: Stop marketing. Start engaging*, Wiley, Chichester

5   75 customer service facts, quotes and statistics: www.helpscout.com/
    75-customer-service-facts-quotes-statistics/ (archived at https://perma.cc/
    GKD8-YLJP)

6   Data never sleeps 9.0, https://www.domo.com/learn/infographic/
    data-never-sleeps-9 (archived at https://perma.cc/BF9T-EU7T)

7   Carvill, M (2018) *Get Social: Social media strategy and tactics for
    leaders*, Kogan Page, London

8   Social media proves to boost employee engagement: www.forbes.com/
    sites/forbesagencycouncil/2018/02/13/social-media-proves-to-boost-
    employee-engagement/ (archived at https://perma.cc/J9Z4-76BJ)

MYTH 28

Oversharing on social media can reveal trade secrets

It's important that provisions are in place to protect the organization, and that employees are clear on their responsibilities and the sanctions that could be enforced if that expected standard is not met.

Social networks and technologies such as blogs, forums and other networked platforms have become increasingly powerful in connecting organizations with customers and, as explored in Myth 13, in connecting businesses with their own employees.

With more than 50 per cent of the world engaged on social networks, for many organizations they are now considered 'business as usual'.

However, given that social media communication is generally far freer and more casual, there's good reason why the cautious are concerned about the challenge and risk of oversharing on social media. Such informality could lead to unintentionally revealing trade secrets for everyone, including competitors, to see.

On the face of it, it sounds simple. Empower the use of social media within organizations and advise employees to be careful about what they share. Provide a clear framework within which to operate alongside clarity on the dos and don'ts, share the organizational guidelines and ensure everything is updated in the employee handbook. Job done. But it isn't this simple. In just the same way that being 'social' is deeply ingrained within the complexities of how we communicate, so too are there complexities in managing the risks associated with this less formal means of communication.

While we're advocates and champions of social media for business, it would be remiss of us not to acknowledge the risks that organizations face when it comes to engaging with social media. This myth explores the risk of oversharing. It looks at some communication frameworks and social media guidelines that while simple, engender trust. It also explores some of the legal positioning and shares insights about what organizations are doing at a practical level to mitigate risk.

Start with the end in mind

Social media activity is pervasive in our everyday lives, so the lines around professional and personal viewpoints, and who is saying what and in what context, can easily become blurred. Of course, the whole idea of social media is to encourage sharing, and yet in certain circumstances, it may be risky or sensitive for employees to talk freely. This includes posting about a new product they are working on, or a new client that they've just landed. Not only is training required when organizations embrace social media, but businesses also need to think through how processes and job roles are to be supported or facilitated by social media. Embracing the opportunities that come with using social media for professional networking, while at the same time safeguarding against any major risks, is something that needs to be considered end-to-end and communicated to employees, ideally in a way that is easily accessible, transparent and clear. For example, take the role of a business development manager. It is highly likely that they will be encouraged to use their own personal social networks to enhance the work they do within the organization. Therefore, it's important to consider the lines of control and ownership around the use of personal social networks – including what happens when employees leave.

The question of who owns the social media accounts is, at the time of writing, being litigated between a bridal designer and her former employer, JLM Couture. While there was an employment contract governing the relationship between employee and employer, it didn't cover social media accounts. When the relationship ended, JLM Couture claimed ownership of the designer's Instagram, TikTok and Pinterest accounts on the basis that she had created them in her capacity as a designer in their employment. The bridal designer is arguing that she created them in her personal capacity, and did not cede ownership by agreeing to use the accounts to market the company's products. This brings to light for employers the importance of clarifying who owns a social media account.[1]

Keeping employees up to speed

In an interview conducted with Kevin Burrowes, Global Clients and Industries Leader at PwC, he suggested PwC should invest in social media training for all employees, with annual exams.[2] Employees would have to pass those exams, with clear sanctions in place when guidelines aren't adhered to. This provides an excellent example of employers taking responsibility not only to train and educate employees, but also to regularly ensure everyone is up to speed through continuous education.

At the time of writing, we'd be hard pushed to find an organization that doesn't have some form of social media guidelines. However, assuming employees have read the guidelines and are clear on the boundaries, organizational expectation and preferences is something that needs to be checked regularly. It's equally wise to sense-check how the guidelines are being communicated. It's unlikely that employees will read and adhere to a complicated, legalese-riddled 38-page document created by a compliance team.

When it comes to social media guidelines, we particularly like the empowered positioning of the ones from Best Buy.[3] The guidelines, entitled 'Be Smart, Be Respectful, Be Human', not only speak to employees as grown-ups, enabling them to use best judgement, but are very clear and succinct. In fact, they fit onto one highly informative page.

Ensuring data security

The speed with which technology is evolving also poses security and risk challenges. The portability of digital devices, growth of flexible working and BYOD (bring your own device) to work schemes, data storage and connections with customers or suppliers on social media all heighten the risk. And when it comes to trade secrets, what may seem like a genuinely innocent conversation on social media could lead to employees disclosing confidential customer data without even realizing they are doing so.

The laws around data security are hugely complex, and differ dependent upon where you are in the world and jurisdictions.[4] That said, while issues related to social media privacy in the workplace are likely to continue, there are some practical things employers can do to engage and educate employees to safeguard data and trade secrets. It's a question of striking a balance between empowering employees to converse, share and network, and doing it within a clear framework of what is and isn't permissible.

Some practical questions to consider:

- Have you set clear expectations? Is there a social media mission statement that articulates clearly how social media is expected to be used within the business and how it aligns with overall business strategy and the role each employee plays?
- Do all employees take social media training? If so, how often is it revisited, and how do you know they've embedded the key learnings – for example, are there exams?

- Do you have clear social media guidelines that are easy to locate and simple to understand? Do they clearly detail the dos and don'ts (in just the same way you may have user-friendly brand guidelines)?
- Are access/login and publishing rights on social media limited to relevant people?
- Do you have resources dedicated to managing and assessing the continuous changes happening within social media to ensure these are communicated swiftly and effectively across the organization?
- Is there a process for onboarding new team members so that they are trained and instantly up to speed with social media guidelines, expectations and dos and don'ts?
- Is there a policy clearly outlining the process for handing over social media account access when an employee leaves?

These questions are by no means prescriptive – our intention is rather to provoke your thinking and to provide a simple baseline from which to sense-check the practicality of your own guidelines and practice.

Conclusion

This is not a myth. If an employee were to overshare on social media, it could indeed reveal trade secrets. Social media sits within employees' work and personal lives and cultivating a social media presence within an organization is increasingly an explicit part of many employees' jobs. It's important that provisions are in place to protect the organization, and that employees are clear on their responsibilities and the sanctions that could be enforced if that expected standard is not met.

Notes

1 Does the employer or employee own those social media accounts? https://shawe.com/eupdate/does-the-employer-or-employee-own-those-social-media-accounts/ (archived at https://perma.cc/URZ8-FRLH)

2 Carvill, M (2018) *Get Social: Social media strategy and tactics for leaders*, Kogan Page, London

3 Best Buy social media policy: https://forums.bestbuy.com/t5/Welcome-News/Best-Buy-Social-Media-Policy/td-p/20492 (archived at https://perma.cc/F9T4-9ZUE)

4 How social media, technology and privacy laws are changing the e-discovery landscape: www.skadden.com/insights/publications/2019/04/quarterly-insights/how-social-media-technology-and-privacy-laws (archived at https://perma.cc/8TRR-YT3X)

MYTH 29

Being active on social media lets me control my digital footprint

Being active online does help you control your active digital footprint, but it's also important to understand how, when, where and why companies are collecting data about you.

Everything someone does online leaves some sort of trace. Every website visited, every transaction, social media post or interaction leaves a trail. This is a fact of digital life, and it's impossible to avoid, but it can be managed. It's very important to understand how this works and to know what kind of trail you are leaving online.

Everything a company or individual does online leaves a trace, and many companies use these traces of online behaviour to target customers. Much of the tracking revolves around identifying people's general patterns of behaviour, desires and opinions online in order to sell them products or services.

Your digital footprint is made up of many different traces of online activity. Posted photos and comments on social media are often among the more visible traces. But everything from shopping online to visiting news and media websites, making Skype calls or sending emails can leave different records.

One of the advantages of actively managing your online presence is that you can influence the form of information that is available about you online. For example, in Myth 6 we talked about responding to criticism online. In this case, providing channels for people to make complaints and resolve disputes will help to mitigate the negative discussions about a business or a brand on other channels.

The same can be true for individuals. As we discussed in the previous two myths, individuals can actively manage the information that is available about themselves online. This means that when a person actively manages and curates this information, choosing the content and the channels, they can make sure they can be in control of their digital footprint.

Active footprints are traces you deliberately leave online. This is information associated with you or your computer, or an online account where you post or publish information.

Passive footprints are traces that you leave behind online without intending to do so, and sometimes without even knowing that you are leaving a trace. This information is collected automatically through the course of your online activities.

Generally, it is advisable for everyone to understand what a digital footprint is, and how your online behaviour affects your online experience. It is especially important for managing professional and corporate reputations. Employers may look for digital footprints of prospective hires. Having a messy footprint can cost people jobs, opportunities and damage professional or corporate reputations.

Having a well-managed footprint can be a great tool for managing professional or corporate reputation. Social media sites let you choose what information to share online and what to make publicly available. A strong and positive professional digital footprint can, and often does, attract job offers, recruiters and positive interaction online.

CASE STUDY   The author's digital footprint

To explain the situation, we decided to do some digging into my digital footprint. If you were to look at my digital footprint, you could find a lot of information just by typing 'Ian MacRae' into a search engine. There's more than one 'Ian MacRae', so by adding a keyword like 'psychologist', 'personality', 'leadership' or 'high potential' you would get more accurate results. You'd probably find my social media profiles, links to books and articles I've written, relevant news stories and media appearances. With a bit of digging you might be able to find a bit more. However, that active digital footprint only scratches the surface of my overall digital footprint.

Most companies with a digital presence collect data from their customers online. Social media companies have a lot more information about me than is publicly available. Utility providers, airlines, banks and department stores have information about all their customers. Mobile applications, emails, loyalty cards and things purchased online contribute to that footprint.

How much of that information can be tracked down? It turns out that because of the EU General Data Protection Regulation (GDPR) every company in the UK or EU must provide copies of the personal data they collect about people. I put together a list of 100 companies that would have personal data about me (the total list would be longer, but I restricted the search to most frequently used and more recent accounts). The process was relatively easy, although extremely time-consuming.

According to GDPR rules, all companies must have a process to provide people with copies of their personal data if requested. Companies have one month to complete the request, where they must provide all the personal data they store about an individual. This data can be anything from a few lines of text to thousands of pages, or vast spreadsheets of data.

Overall, most companies were quick, responsive and friendly. Ninety-three per cent of the companies contacted did provide copies of my personal data they held, and one of the companies that didn't respond went bust shortly after my request, so would not be expected to complete it.

Results

Based on the results of the GDPR requests, I found I could categorize companies into three general trends in their data collection activities. Where companies did not respond (including Virgin Media, NowTV and Principal Hotel Group) I assumed that the data collection they describe on their privacy policy was accurate:

1 **Very minimal data collection.** Most companies (72 per cent) collected and stored surprisingly little personal data. Many of the companies such as retail stores, train companies, some loyalty card providers and even mobile phone applications were only collecting and storing minimal personal data. Most retail and department stores, for example, only stored purchase history and basic personal contact details.

2 **Customer profiling in line with business.** A smaller segment of companies (19 per cent) had more detailed personal information, or more detailed consumer profiles. These were companies such as supermarkets and some loyalty cards (Nectar), airlines, video games companies and financial institutions. While these companies did store more personal information, it was an entirely reasonable amount of data and in some cases data that would be covered by other regulatory requirements. For example, streaming websites stored viewing preferences and utility companies had usage history and details, along with communication logs.

3 **Expansive data collection.** A much smaller proportion (9 per cent) of the companies collected and stored vast

amounts of personal data about me. The usual suspects had a disproportionate amount of personal data: Google, Amazon, Apple, Facebook and Twitter. This small minority of companies stored more than 99 per cent of the personal data.

It's not entirely unreasonable that social media companies would have huge amounts of data, because the purpose of social media companies is to store personal information and communication online. Providing a digital communications platform involves collecting and storing huge amounts of data. It is the business model, and necessary for the service they provide. The same is true for internet service providers, who are required by law to store customers' internet records for a year. On the surface, this is not necessarily a problem. However, one of the major concerns is when they start collecting data that is not necessary or collecting data without informed consent.

Interestingly, because I use the privacy and security tools that will be discussed in Myth 30, there were large amounts of inaccurate data. The companies where I left a much larger, passive footprint had more inaccuracies in their data. That's because the privacy tools prevent these companies from automatically collecting accurate personal data such as my location. For example, Twitter had my device location and time zone set as 'Arizona' and my Google location history had extensive location history in Florida (I have never been to Arizona or Florida).

As greater numbers of people use these fairly cheap and simple privacy tools (see Myth 30), it becomes much more difficult for these companies that collect vast amounts of data to automatically hoover up detailed personal data from people.

Very personal data

Companies and applications that collect the most amount of data are also the companies that run the risk of collecting data that is too personal. It is easy to forget how significant this data collection is when it happens passively. For example, Google collects detailed location history when you use products like Google Maps. This can be a convenient tool for day-to-day use, but when the data is compiled over the years it provides a surprising level of insight into someone's individual behaviour.

From Google maps you can create a plot a diagram that shows your Google location history. The map will be shaded based on your Google location history. It's possible. It is recorded as specific geographic coordinates and times, so the data is available minute-by-minute and street-by-street. It even estimates how you are travelling (eg 'on foot', 'in vehicle' or 'on bicycle'). My Google location history had over 1 million lines of data (1,048,575), but if you regularly use additional location-based products like Fitbit, this amount of data will be substantially higher.

A full, but fragmented picture

The results may be surprising: most companies or organizations only collect minimal personal data, largely in line with the basic and necessary information I would expect them to have, such as previous transactions, communication history and marketing preferences.

Putting all the information together from different companies, there was a substantial amount of data that could be combined to create a very detailed look into my daily life, personal behaviour, consumer preferences, spending patterns and activity. Since most of the data was scattered between many different companies, the personal data from 91 per cent of the more modest data collectors did not reveal very much taken in isolation. But if you put all the data together, you could combine a substantial amount of information including scheduling, contact lists, online communication, household energy use, purchase histories, film, TV and pop culture interests, and much more.

However, this data was mostly fragmented. Except for the larger data collectors, most companies only had a small amount of personal data that was not particularly concerning or unreasonable in scale. Supermarkets can be expected to understand your food shopping habits, airlines to have your flight history, your gym to have your activity history, and your bank should know where you are spending your money and how much you make.

There were two areas of concern:

- Social media and technology companies collect a vast amount of data automatically, and in many cases, this is difficult or impossible to control. Most smartphones and applications are designed to automatically share personal data. This means that location data is probably available for most people who regularly use a smartphone. For anyone that uses their phone to track things like their exercise, sleep schedule or food intake, the data is likely to be even more comprehensive. Remember what we said in previous myths: if the product or service is free, then you are probably not the customer – your data is the product.

- I generally avoid smartphone applications that collect unnecessary amounts of personal data, and have added security applications on my smartphone to minimize the amount of data that is collected without my consent. Social media smartphone applications are terrible offenders in this area. Mobile games often hoover up unnecessary data and are a significant privacy concern.[1,2,3] There are significant concerns around newer and emerging applications such as those that swap, change or enhance people's faces – concerns that in the longer term these will be used for facial recognition or developing deepfake technology.[4]

Conclusion

Being active online does help you control your active digital footprint, but it's also important to understand how, when, where and why companies are collecting data about you.

Shaping the trail of data you leave online is important. It can change the way people talk about, and interact with, a business. For individuals, it can affect everything from your employment prospects and credit rating to the news, media and advertising you are presented with.

Notes

1 Your digital footprint matters: https://perma.cc/BQ5U-CA56
2 Data privacy and security: Why mobile apps are the new weak link: www.infosecurity-magazine.com/next-gen-infosec/privacy-mobile-apps-weak-link-1-1 (archived at https://perma.cc/D9UW-24LX)
3 How game apps that captivate kids have been collecting their data: www.nytimes.com/interactive/2018/09/12/technology/kids-apps-data-privacy-google-twitter.html (archived at https://perma.cc/D9Z5-96MQ)
4 China's red-hot face-swapping app provokes privacy concern: www.bloomberg.com/news/articles/2019-09-02/china-s-red-hot-face-swapping-app-provokes-privacy-concern (archived at https://perma.cc/6CAB-PEN4)

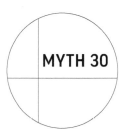

Social networks will protect my data

Even those companies with the most sophisticated cybersecurity measures in place cannot promise to protect your data.

How much can you trust the greediest and most prolific data gatherers with your data? Should you trust the privacy and security measures of tech giants like Meta, Microsoft, Google, Bytedance, Tencent and Apple to protect your personal data? Or should you be taking additional steps to protect your own information?

Every year companies lose people's data, and seem to break records with every new breach.[1,2] Major companies such as LinkedIn, Apple, Microsoft, Mimecast, Facebook, Volkswagen, T-Mobile, Panasonic and CNA Financial all suffered data breaches in 2021.[3,4,5] In January 2022, security consultants IT Governance reported that over 5.1 billion electronic records had been breached.[6]

Let's assume that all social media companies are completely committed to data protection, security and privacy. You may or may not think that is a safe assumption, but even if it is the case, any company, even those with the most sophisticated cybersecurity countermeasures, will suffer from accidental leaks, hacks or technical problems at some point in time.[7]

Fortunately, the tools and techniques for keeping yourself and your data safe online are relatively cheap, accessible and easy to use. We outline some of the best options below, and highly recommend using these, if you do not already.

Data protection tools and techniques

Regular software updates

This is one of the easiest and most important steps to keeping your devices safe. Make sure to regularly update the software on your devices. In many cases, and on most new devices, this is done automatically.

Keeping your software updated protects your devices from known viruses and potential problems. It won't protect against every threat, but it is an important first step. Many of the data breaches of companies and even governmental departments have resulted from vulnerabilities in out-of-date software.

Antivirus software

Your device will include some security elements, and keeping the software updated as mentioned in the previous point will help to keep your devices secure. However, dedicated antivirus software can help to keep your devices protected much more effectively than the manufacturer of the device you are using. They tend to offer better protection by scanning files on your device that could be harmful, blocking potentially malicious websites.

There are plenty of companies offering relatively inexpensive and user-friendly antivirus software. Articles in magazines such as *TechRadar* or *PCMag* provide useful lists of recommended antivirus software for different devices.

Private browsing

Private browsing is one of the most basic features for limiting the amount of personal data you share while online. Most browsers come with a built-in 'private', or 'incognito' feature.

When you're in a private browsing window, your computer does not store your own search history, files you've downloaded, or information you are accessing online. Essentially, it means your computer forgets everything you did during the private browsing session after you close the window. What it does not do is stop anyone else from collecting your data. The searches you make in a search engine can still be stored by the activity of other applications, and often will be.

This makes private browsing a limited way to reduce personal information sharing, but it does mean less data is stored on your own device.

Password managers

Password managers are a simple step everyone can take to protect their privacy and security online. If there is one piece of advice you take away from this myth, let it be to start using a password manager.

One of the biggest security threats online is reusing the same email address or username and password across many different sites. Most people know they shouldn't do this, but do it anyway. Every year when lists of the most popular passwords are published, there is little change. Up until recently, the most common password was 'password', although it is now in second place, and an astounding number of people still choose easy-to-crack variants such as '123456', 'querty', 'admin', 'abc123' or 'iloveyou'. Topical passwords are always popular too. At the time of writing in 2022, 'trump', 'biden', 'sourdough', 'pokemon' and variations on 'coronavirus' are all up there.[8]

Please do not do this. There are plenty of very good, highly secure companies that offer password managers, including Lastpass or 1Password. A password manager will generate random passwords for each of the different sites you use, and store this information securely. They are easy to use, and typically come with apps for your computer and phone that will autocomplete your usernames and passwords for all of your different logins.

Of course, you should have one master password to log in to the password manager that is both secure (not 123456), relatively easy to remember and not used anywhere else. Usernames and passwords get hacked, leaked or guessed all the time. Password managers can take some getting used to, but it is one of the quickest and most effective ways to protect yourself and your data online.

Identifying data breaches

Companies are not always quick to disclose when they have lost people's data. They should immediately inform everyone who has been affected, but the reality is that sometimes the people who could be the most affected are the last to find out. If your username and password have been stolen from a website you use, the best thing to do is immediately change that password, and make sure you also change it anywhere else you may have used it.

There's a very good free service that alerts you if there have been any data breaches associated with your email account, called Have I Been Pwned?[9] You can subscribe using your email address to be alerted if and when that email address is associated with any data leaks or breaches. It doesn't require any personal information other than your email address, which most people feel comfortable handing out. Avoid similar services that ask for your password or other sensitive information.

Virtual private networks

Typically, when you are online, most of your activity will be connected with you through your Internet Protocol (IP) address. This means that every website you visit gets a number to identify you. This connects you to your internet service provider and physical location. Many companies will track your activity online (your internet provider keeps a log of every website you have visited over the last year). Social media sites are among the worst offenders, tracking much of your online activity even when you are not on their site.

A virtual private network (VPN) essentially uses a highly encrypted connection and puts all the information you are sending into a black box. About 31 per cent of internet users now connect through a VPN.[10] Using a VPN restricts external parties or companies from being able to 'listen in' on your online activity. Whenever you are sending or receiving information, especially related to business activities, client or customer data, private communications, or confidential documents, it is sent privately and securely. By putting it all in that secure VPN black box, it keeps your personal or private data secure and private.

There are plenty of companies that offer VPN services quite inexpensively. There are some free options, but these are usually too slow to be practical.

Two-factor authentication

An increasing number of companies that hold important data or have access to financial accounts are moving to two-factor authentication. Most banks now use a variety of two-factor authentication methods to keep their customers' accounts more secure. Methods vary, but it essentially means that two different security steps are required to access an account. This can include email, text or phone call verification as well as a password, making it more difficult for unauthorized users to access people's accounts.

As well as financial accounts, it is advisable to have two-factor authentication on any accounts that hold personal, sensitive or security information, or which themselves could be used to reset a lost password or as a second factor in authentication, such as email accounts.

Physical authentication devices

Physical authentication is a type of authentication that requires a material (not digital) security step. It can be a device that creates a numerical or visual code that can be used to log in to accounts, or one which has a smart chip that needs to be connected to another device as a security measure. These are typically plugged into a USB or audio port, but can also use a wireless connection.

Essentially, these protect devices or accounts by making sure no one can access them without the physical token. This can take a bit longer to set up, and can cause problems if you misplace the physical token. It does, however, offer a much stronger level of security for accounts that are important to keep secure.

Conclusion

Even those companies with the most sophisticated cyber-security measures in place cannot promise to protect your data. Fortunately, you can protect your security and your company's security by taking a few simple steps. Organizations should also take steps to teach their employees about the importance of staying secure online as more and more business communications and processes move into digital spaces.

Notes

1　Data breaches keep happening. So why don't you do something? www.nytimes.com/2018/08/01/technology/data-breaches.html (archived at https://perma.cc/E4CP-PFHB)

2　Millions of Facebook user records exposed in data breach: www.telegraph.co.uk/technology/2019/04/03/millions-facebook-user-records-exposed-data-breach (archived at https://perma.cc/7MLN-VXA7)

3　An update on report of scraped data: https://news.linkedin.com/2021/june/an-update-from-linkedin (archived at https://perma.cc/G262-6Q77)

4　Apple data breaches: Full timeline through 2022: https://firewalltimes.com/apple-data-breach-timeline/ (archived at https://perma.cc/DJS5-YHVT)

5　The biggest data breaches, hacks of 2021: https://www.zdnet.com/article/the-biggest-data-breaches-of-2021/ (archived at https://perma.cc/MD5Z-FF33)

6　Data breaches and cyber attacks in 2021: 5.1 billion breached records: https://www.itgovernance.co.uk/blog/data-breaches-and-cyber-attacks-in-2021-5-1-billion-breached-records (archived at https://perma.cc/X7E6-8SFP)

7　Americans and cybersecurity: www.pewinternet.org/2017/01/26/americans-and-cybersecurity (archived at https://perma.cc/6649-G2RC)

8　SpyCloud 2021 Annual Credential Exposure Report: https://spycloud.com/resource/2021-annual-credential-exposure-report/ (archived at https://perma.cc/LVE9-SGY4)

9　Have I been pwned? https://haveibeenpwned.com (archived at https://perma.cc/AYG8-HK6M)

10　VPN statistics for 2022: https://dataprot.net/statistics/vpn-statistics/ (archived at https://perma.cc/P86R-MZJZ)

Index

Other titles in the Myths series

ISBN: 9781398607781   ISBN: 9781398607828   ISBN: 9781398608573

ISBN: 9781398608153   ISBN: 9781398608276   ISBN: 9781398607743

CPSIA information can be obtained
at www.ICGtesting.com
Printed in the USA
BVHW021917270922
648097BV00007B/21